INSIGHT ⊙ GUIDES

EXPLORE

KUALA LUMPUR

D0226834

⊙ Walking Eye App

YOUR FREE EBOOK AVAILABLE THROUGH THE WALKING EYE APP

Your guide now includes a free eBook to your chosen destination, for the same great price as before. Simply download the Walking Eye App from the App Store or Google Play to access your free eBook.

HOW THE WALKING EYE APP WORKS

Through the Walking Eye App, you can purchase a range of eBooks and destination content. However, when you buy this book, you can download the corresponding eBook for free. Just see below in the grey panel where to find your free content and then scan the QR code at the bottom of this page.

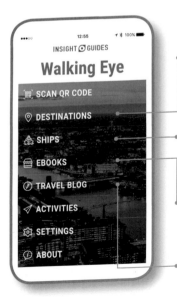

Destinations: Download essential destination content featuring recommended sights and attractions, restaurants, hotels and an A–Z of practical information, all available for purchase.

Ships: Interested in ship reviews? Find independent reviews of river and ocean ships in this section, all available for purchase.

eBooks: You can download your free accompanying digital version of this guide here. You will also find a whole range of other eBooks, all available for purchase.

Free access to travel-related blog articles about different destinations, updated on a daily basis.

HOW THE EBOOKS WORK

The eBooks are provided in EPUB file format. Please note that you will need an eBook reader installed on your device to open the file. Many devices come with this as standard, but you may still need to install one manually from Google Play.

The eBook content is identical to the content in the printed guide.

HOW TO DOWNLOAD THE WALKING EYE APP

1. Download the Walking Eye App from the App Store or Google Play.
2. Open the app and select the scanning function from the main menu.
3. Scan the QR code on this page – you will then be asked a security question to verify ownership of the book.
4. Once this has been verified, you will see your eBook in the purchased ebook section, where you will be able to download it.

Other destination apps and eBooks are available for purchase separately or are free with the purchase of the Insight Guide book.

CONTENTS

ARCHITECTURE

The contemporary Petronas Twin Towers (route 3) contrast with the Mughal-style Sultan Abdul Samad Building (route 1), while tradition is preserved in the headman's house, Rumah Penghulu Abu Seman (route 7).

RECOMMENDED ROUTES FOR...

ARTS BUFFS

Discover historical artefacts at the Museum of Asian Art (route 15) and the Bank Negara Museum and Art Gallery (route 6), while contemporary art can be appreciated at the Petronas Gallery and Ilham Gallery (both route 3).

HIDDEN GEMS

Surprising discoveries can be found in the most unexpected of places. These include three floors of cafés and art in a crumbling shop house (route 2), a Buddhist temple back-to-back with a red light district (route 5), an adventure cave in a temple complex (route 8) and the Conservatory of Rare Plants and Orchids in a sleepy suburb (route 15).

FAMILIES WITH KIDS

Petrosains makes the oil and gas industry a ton of fun (route 3). Visit KLCC Park for its giant playground and wading pool (route 3). Get close to Asian elephants at Kuala Gandah (route 13). Theme park fans should head to Sunway Lagoon (route 15).

FESTIVALS

Prayers, decorations and festive food abound during festivals, such as the Chinese New Year in Petaling Street and Bukit Bintang (routes 2 and 7), Wesak Day in Brickfields (route 5) and the Hindu Thaipusam celebration in Batu Caves (route 8).

FOOD AND DRINK

Sample Malaysians' favourite breakfast of *nasi lemak* (coconut rice) at Restaurant Rebung Chef Ismail (route 4), the KL speciality of Hokkien *mee* at Seng Kee Restaurant (route 2), Hainanese chicken chop at the Coliseum (route 6) and a great Indian vegetarian spread at Vishal Food and Catering (route 5).

ESCAPING THE CROWDS

Escape the frenetic city pace; head to the leafy Taman Botani Perdana or the fountain courtyard at the Islamic Arts Museum (route 4). Find peace in the open spaces of the National Mosque (route 1) and the secluded Guan Di Temple (route 2).

RAINFOREST ENCOUNTERS

Amazing rainforest discoveries include lowland forest canopies at the Canopy Walkway (route 9), riverine vegetation at Chiling Waterfall (route 10), mangroves and mudflats at the Kuala Selangor Nature Park (route 14) and misty montane habitats at Fraser's Hill (route 11).

INTRODUCTION

An introduction to Kuala Lumpur's geography, customs and culture, plus illuminating background information on cuisine, history and what to do when you're there.

Petronas Twin Towers

EXPLORE KUALA LUMPUR

Kuala Lumpur was never the centre of an ancient civilisation. Yet in its short lifespan, it has become a major player in Southeast Asia, embracing globalisation yet retaining its distinctly multi-ethnic cadences.

Just 160 years ago, Kuala Lumpur – or KL, as it is popularly known – was nothing more than marsh, muck and mudbank. Today, it is a cosmopolitan, wired commercial centre, learned in the street smarts of the Western world and driven by capitalism and globalisation. Yet, the city is also steeped in the rich and variegated traditions of Malay, Chinese, Indian and other cultures. This multilayered persona is evident in everything from architecture and music to festivals and KL-ites' favourite preoccupation – food.

DEVELOPMENT

In 1857, an expedition of Chinese tin miners headed up the Klang River from Pengkalan Batu (now Port Klang). When they arrived at the confluence of the Klang and Gombak rivers, they had to stop as the rivers were too shallow to accommodate their fully laden flotilla. Their resting place was nothing more than a tiny hamlet nestled in a quagmire of mud. Appropriately, the miners called the settlement Kuala Lumpur – meaning 'muddy confluence'.

Tin was eventually found in Ampang, upstream of KL, but because the rivers were too shallow, KL remained a convenient staging point for supplies and ore. Buoyed by high tin prices, the settlement developed into a booming mining town by the 1860s.

19th Century

The miners were Chinese immigrants who came under community leaders called the 'Kapitan Cina'. The most illustrious was Yap Ah Loy, a Hakka immigrant, who rebuilt KL at least three times, once after the Selangor Civil War and twice after the great fire of 1881, and governed it like his own little kingdom until the first British Resident (ruler) turned up in 1880.

The next major personality was Frank Swettenham, the Resident of Selangor appointed in 1882. Together with Yap, he replaced the shanties and huts that formed much of KL with brick structures, and constructed the KL–Klang railway link, ending the city's dependence on the river.

An active policy of emigration and the encouragement of agriculture on its periphery increased the Malay

KL City Gallery

and Indian populations while diminishing the economic control wielded by Chinese migrants. In 1896 KL was declared capital of the Federated Malay States. Both world wars did little damage to the city, and in 1963, KL became the capital of Malaysia. The city was declared a Federal Territory in 1974. Since then, KL has bloomed into one of the most modern cities in Southeast Asia.

MODERN KUALA LUMPUR

In the 1990s, KL became the site for a building boom of massive skyscrapers, symbols of Malaysia's aspirations

Bukit Nenas

to gain developed nation status. The most significant were the Petronas Twin Towers. These days, it is the lack of space that is resulting in vertical building. In 1999, the executive and judicial branches of the federal government moved to Putrajaya but KL has remained the seat of Parliament. It is also the country's financial and commercial centre.

KL's urban sophistication does give it an international feel. Some visitors like this, as it provides them with enough global stamps of familiarity to take to the city easily. However, in some areas, basic infrastructure has simply not kept pace with the rest of the city's unbridled growth. The traffic jams, pollution, flash floods and imperviousness to heritage testify to this.

There are, however, pockets of the old KL that are still evident. So you may come across a colourful Hindu temple at a busy junction, or a row of pre-war shophouses behind a ritzy mall, while the sound of squawking chickens could lead you to a fresh-produce market that has existed for generations.

Meanwhile, a 10-year one-billion-ringgit federal programme, intended to help Malaysia achieve developed nation status by 2020, has a specific focus on KL and the Klang Valley. It is attracting investors, improving public transport, making the city greener, creating a pedestrian network, cleaning up the waterways and rejuvenating riverside infrastructure and communities.

Eating at a hawker stall

ORIENTATION

KL is situated about halfway down the west coast of the peninsula and 35km (22 miles) inland. It is bordered on the east by the Titiwangsa Mountains and sits in the Klang river basin. A metropolis with an area of about 234sq km (90sq miles), KL anchors a conurbation known as the Klang Valley, which roughly follows the Klang River that empties into the Straits of Malacca. The Klang Valley encompasses cities like Petaling Jaya and Klang, and the federal administrative capital of Putrajaya.

Right in the old heart of KL is the colonial core around the Padang, where the Europeans used to hang out; the new heart east of that is the KL City Centre (KLCC), home to the Petronas Twin Towers. Next to the old heart is Petaling Street and, in the north, Masjid India and Jalan Tuanku Abdul Rahman. South of the KLCC is the shopping and commercial centre of Bukit Bintang, which sits in the financial and commercial area known as the Golden Triangle.

Navigating the City

Most attractions are accessible on foot, and walking is the quickest way to get around during the gridlock weekday rush hours of 7–9am and 5–8pm. To travel between attractions that are further apart, take the air-conditioned rail systems or free bus. These also take you to attractions outside of the city centre. Alternatively, taxis are cheap, so book one for the day. Many of the attractions covered in this guide are also part of guided tours from KL.

Rainy streets and traffic at Bukit Bintang

Portraits on display

Chinatown

A MELTING POT

KL has the country's highest per capita GDP and an employment-to-population ratio twice that of other metropolitan areas. Its population of over 1.8 million swells to over 2.5 million in the daytime when workers commute from the Klang Valley. A large migrant labour force plays an indispensable role in its economy. KL-ites tend to manifest many of the traits of an urbanised population. They have a more international outlook compared to residents in the rest of the country and tend to be better travelled and are more influenced by global trends.

Large numbers of Chinese started settling in KL in the 19th century, even-

---

DON'T LEAVE KUALA LUMPUR WITHOUT...

Taking a selfie with the Petronas Twin Towers. Find a good angle from the Suria Esplanade, the KLCC Park or the KL Tower to take a selfie with these 88-storey steel wonders. See page 42.

Walking the heritage quarter. Take a stroll around the domes and minarets of Mughal architecture for an intimate look at the colonial idea of a Far Eastern administrative centre. See page 30.

Savouring street food. Head to the hawker stalls in Bukit Bintang to try some local delicacies. These operate late into the night and whip up favourites as the signature KL *Hokkien Mee* (stir-fried noodles). See page 66.

Experiencing Chinese temples. The numerous Buddhist and Taoist temples in the Petaling Street area are wonderful to pop in and out of. Note the varied statues of deities as well as temple adornments. See page 39.

Learning about elephants. Learn about Asian elephant conservation at the Kuala Gandah Elephant Conservation Centre, where you can watch a short film about threats to them, see them up-close and interact with them. See page 83.

Climbing to a limestone temple. Walk up the 272 steps to visit the ethereal Batu Caves Hindu temple, located in a limestone massif. At its foot is the world's largest statue of the Hindu deity Murugan. See page 68.

Strolling through a pasar malam. Night markets are fun and full of colour and provide a chance to rub shoulders with the locals. At Brickfields, *pasar malam* stalls are set up on an old street full of places of worship. See page 19.

Admiring local art. Works by local artists can be appreciated at various art galleries in the city, including the beautiful spaces that are the Galeri Petronas and Ilham Gallery in the KLCC area. See page 44.

Being among the treetops. Head to the Forest Research Institute, dedicated to the study of tropical forests, and go on the Canopy Walkway, 30 metres above the forest floor to enjoy being among huge trees. See page 70.

tually dominating commerce. Today, they make up 43 per cent of KL's population. Malays make up 46 percent; large numbers migrated from the rural areas in the 1970s–80s for economic reasons. Most work in the service and government sectors. About 10 percent of KL-ites are Indians who arrived in the 19th century as manual labour-

St Mary's Cathedral

ers, mainly from South India, but a fair sprinkling of Northerners, notably Punjabis, Sikhs and Gujeratis, came to KL for business.

While core ethnic values are largely preserved, especially in religion and marriage, borrowings and adaptations are rampant and imaginative in everything from language and dress to food and social mores. Growing affluence and the common pursuit of material gains also tend to level out differences. On any given street, you will see Chinese and Malay businessmen in shirtsleeves and ties sweat over a curry lunch at an Indian Muslim restaurant. At weekends nightclubs are filled with trendy 20- and 30-somethings pulsating to EDM, even while some in the group might abstain from alcohol or beef for religious purposes.

A TRADITIONAL SPIRIT

All Malays are Muslim. Constitutionally, Islam is Malaysia's official religion, though freedom of religion is assured for the other faiths. The main religions practised are Islam, Buddhism, Taoism and Christianity. Places of worship of different faiths co-exist while cultural and religious festivals are celebrated freely. Malaysia projects an image of a moderate Muslim nation in a troubled post-9/11 world, although global political tensions are stoking a growing Islamic conservatism and ethnic disharmony.

Merdeka Square

TOP TIPS

Pack flip-flops or slip-ons. If you plan to visit places of worship, you will need to leave your shoes outside. These will be easier to remove and put back on, and are also less worthy of being stolen.

No pork please. Pork is never served in Muslim eateries and rarely served in hotel restaurants, so food advertised in your breakfast buffet as 'bacon' is usually beef, and 'ham', chicken.

Rooftop bars. Head up to one of the numerous rooftop bars at sunset to enjoy a wine or beer as the city lights come on. Many bars are angled to have views of the Petronas Twin Towers or the KL Tower, sometimes both.

Discount travel and entry. Children under seven years of age ride free on public transport and those under 12 are entitled to discounted entrance fees. Senior citizens pay half price for public transport but will need to get a concession card from the station. Some theatres offer concession prices for children and pensioners.

Friday prayer time. The Muslim Friday prayer time is from 12.45–2.30pm, and can be tricky as government offices, together with some shops and eateries, operate a reduced service, or even close altogether, as the men go to pray.

King of fruits. The seasonal durian is Malaysians' favourite fruit. Adventurous tourists should give it a go, but be warned that the smell and the texture can be challenging. Hotels are strict about bringing it indoors – look out for the no durian sign.

Cheap tickets. Tickets for the Malaysian Philharmonic Orchestra's matinee concerts can go for as little as RM30. The orchestra also has interesting concerts for children as part of its 'Family Fun Days' programme.

Pedestrian unfriendly. Be careful at pedestrian crossings as drivers don't pay much attention to people wishing to cross, even if the green pedestrian crossing signal is green. Many signals also don't work, so be prepared to dash across streets once you work out the traffic flow.

Smokers. Smokers have it good in KL, with the freedom to smoke anywhere that is not air-conditioned, and also in air-conditioned bars. If you grab an inside table in an eatery, you'll have a better chance of not getting smoked out.

Bargaining. When shopping at markets, shop around to see what the average price is, then, especially in tourist areas such as Petaling Street, offer a price that is at least 50 percent less than the asking price, before settling on an amount that is a little higher.

Hindu temples. These are busiest in the early morning and evening when the curtain concealing the statue of the main deity is unveiled and bathed by the priest, who also conducts prayers.

Travel off-peak. The northern hemisphere summer months are peak tourist periods in KL. Everything is cheaper outside this period. The monsoon months, from November to January, are also cooler.

Chicken satay

FOOD AND DRINK

KL is probably not the best place to be on a diet. The variety is endless, the portions large and the prices reasonable. Choose from Malay, Chinese, Indian and Nonya food, as well as international cuisines and fusion fare.

Drawn by the economic magnet of KL, Malaysians from all over the country have settled in the city, bringing with them cuisines of their own. Regional specialities are easily available, but so are innovations. These include 'beef bacon' to meet *halal* needs, Chinese-style stir-fried vegetables on an Indian menu, and contemporary Asian fare featuring a touch of the European. Beer is available in most non-Muslim eateries, and wine menus are good in the fancier restaurants.

MALAY CUISINE

A cornucopia of herbs and spices such as lemon grass, *galangal* and turmeric imparts a heady bouquet to Malay food. *Nasi lemak*, rice cooked in coconut milk and served with condiments like peanuts, fried anchovies, cucumber and *sambal* chilli, is a breakfast favourite. Another popular treat is *satay*: skewers of marinated meat charcoal-grilled and served with peanut sauce and rice cakes.

The mainstay is the meal of plain white rice accompanied by side dishes such as *rendang*, a dry beef curry; *kacang sambal goreng*, long beans fried with chilli paste and bean curd; and *kangkung*

(water spinach) stir-fried with *belacan* (shrimp paste).

Malay food has its share of regional innovations. Food from the east coast tends to be sweeter, while that from the south has Arabic influences, whereas northern food has Thai accents.

CHINESE CUISINE

Malaysia's Chinese immigrants hail from the southern provinces of China, and today belong to such dialect groups as the Cantonese, Hokkiens, Hainanese, Hakkas and Teochews.

From the Cantonese come favourites such as *char siu* (barbecued pork), dim sum and a refined banquet cuisine known for its delicate flavours. Representative of Hokkien street food is *Hokkien mee*, thick yellow wheat noodles fried in soy sauce with pork, prawns and squid. Another Hokkien dish is *bak kut teh*, a soup of herbs and pork ribs. Teochews are most famous for their plain rice gruel eaten with salty, preserved food, as well as richer fare like braised goose and creamy yam custard.

Hakkas originated *yong tau fu*, an assortment of bean curd and vegetables

Nasi kandar   *Fried fish at the market*

stuffed with fish and meat paste. Many Hainanese immigrants worked as cooks for the British, and from them come Chinese-influenced 'Western' dishes such as chicken chop with Worcestershire sauce.

NONYA CUISINE

Nonya, or Peranakan, food is similar to Malay food but has decidedly Chinese twists. Complex spice pastes are painstakingly pounded by hand, and *kuih*, or sweet confections, are very time-consuming to prepare. Standards include *lemak nanas* (pineapple curry) or *kuah lada* (pepper curry), which are more Malay in character, while dishes like *pongteh*, a salty-sweet gravy redolent of soy bean paste, are more Chinese.

INDIAN CUISINE

The early Indian immigrants came mainly from South India. They brought with them griddle-cooked breads like *roti canai* and *thosai*, and spicy curries, and the tradition of using the hand to eat food heaped on banana leaves.

In the earlier years, Indian Muslim hawkers would carry rice (*nasi*) and curry in two baskets balanced on a *kandar*, or pole, to cater to labourers. This is how the curry-focused *nasi kandar* cuisine came about; it can now be found in just about every coffee shop.

The mainstays of North Indian cuisine are tandoori chicken and *naan*, now available even in casual eateries, while the finer dishes of the maharajahs are served in sumptuously appointed restaurants.

WHERE TO EAT

The gradual sophistication of the city's palate has spawned a new breed of hipster cafés, bistros, food trucks and fine-dining restaurants offering European and Asian cuisines. But the unassuming stars of the dining scene are still the hawker stalls and coffee shops serving humble local specialities.

Open-Air Dining

Supper is KL-ites' favourite end to an evening, with many thronging hawker stalls and *mamak* eateries (Indian Muslim stalls) late at night. These offer lots of local colour and everything from Indian *roti canai* to fried Chinese-style noodles.

Open-air hawker centres are located all over the city and some of the larger ones are in Petaling Street (Chinese food); Jalan Alor (mostly Chinese); Kampung Baru (mostly Malay food); and Jalan Imbi (Chinese). Meanwhile, 24-hour *mamak* joints are everywhere.

Food and Drink Prices

Price per person for a three-course meal without drinks:

$$$$ = over RM100
$$$ = RM70–100
$$ = RM30–70
$ = below RM30

Starhill Gallery

SHOPPING

At first glance, it may seem that KL's retail scene is all about designer boutiques and ritzy malls. But there are also crafts and cultural finds, street markets and ethnic neighbourhoods, which appeal to all kinds of shoppers.

With its numerous luxurious malls and designer boutiques, KL is a veritable shopper's paradise; in fact, the Klang Valley is home to over 150 malls.

They might not have the variety of Singapore or Hong Kong but there is a wide enough selection of everything from luxury brands to cheap products. At the same time, there is plenty to keep craft collectors and bargain hunters happy. Although the law requires retail outlets to affix price tags on all goods sold, bargaining is still an integral part of the Malaysian shopping experience, so you should be prepared to haggle. The exception is in department stores and boutiques, where prices are fixed.

SHOPPING MALLS

For better quality and designer labels, the best bets are the large shopping complexes. The malls offer all kinds of goods, from books and IT products to cameras. But its real draw is fashion; prices for haute couture designer wear and Malaysian-designed apparel and other accessories are very reasonable. Many malls offer tourist privilege cards, which you just sign up for with your pass-port, and can use to get discounts for purchases and F&B. Selected outlets allow GST claims for when you leave the country, so keep the receipts.

The **Bukit Bintang** area is the city's undisputed consumer hub, with a gamut of retail offerings from luxurious goods in **Starhill Gallery** and **Pavilion Kuala Lumpur** (see page 65) to funky, affordable streetwear in **Sungei Wang Plaza** (see page 66).

Many shopping centres are worlds unto their own. Other than boutiques and department stores, they come complete with cineplexes, restaurants and hyper-markets. Example of this include **Suria KLCC** (see page 44) at the base of the Petronas Twin Towers. Further afield from the city centre, air-conditioned retail options that make worthwhile excursions include the high-end **Bangsar Shopping Centre** and **Bangsar Village** (see page 52) in Bangsar and **Sunway Pyramid** (see page 90) in Petaling Jaya.

MARKETS

Despite the profusion of mega malls in the city, traditional markets still have their loyal clientele, and are colour-

Chinatown at night

ful repositories of activity, sounds and smells. Fresh-produce markets, good places to buy local fruits and curry pastes, generally operate from 5am until noon. One of the city's oldest is the **Petaling Street Market** (see page 38).

Night Markets

Meanwhile, *pasar malam*, or night markets, are usually set up around 6pm. They are itinerant, so check with your hotel or the City Hall (www.dbkl.com.my). Mingle with the locals as they haggle over fresh produce, cheap clothing and toys and household goods; sample local snacks or hawker food. Worth visiting are the *pasar malam* along **Jalan Telawi** in Bangsar (Sunday); along **Lorong Tuanku Abdul Rahman** (Saturday) in the Masjid India area; and along **Jalan Berhala** in Brickfields (Thursday). The most famous *pasar malam* in KL is the **Petaling Street Bazaar** (see page 38), which has become an institution in its own right.

Flea Markets

Weekend bazaars are a great place to buy local and hand-made products, from soaps to clothes and cookies to art. The best place for second-hand stuff is the **Amcorp Mall Flea Market** in Petaling Jaya (www.facebook.com/amcorpmall official), while high-end products can be found at the **Bangsar Shopping Centre** (www.facebook.com/BangsarShopping Centre). Once every two months, over 100 vendors gather at the **Jaya One Mall** in Petaling Jaya (www.facebook.

com/marketsmy), organised by pop-up space **Pop @ Jaya One**, which is also worth checking out. Creative art markets with products and performances by local artists include the **Fuyoh Art Bazaar**, held every final weekend at the **Publika Mall** (www.facebook.com/ artrowpublika) and **Art for Grabs**, held quarterly in various locations (www.facebook.com/artforgrabs)

HANDICRAFTS

Move away from the big brands in contemporary malls and you will discover the cultural side of KL's shopping landscape.

Traditional Fabrics

Handed down from the grand courts of Kelantan in the Peninsula's east coast, *songket* fabric is a display of dramatic handwoven tradition featuring intricate tapestry inlaid with gold and metallic threads. Its richness makes it more suitable as formal and ceremonial attire. The rich fabric is also frequently made into formal jackets, evening wear and handbags and shoes.

Batik, the less glamorous cousin of *songket*, has more appeal because of its versatility, durability and lower price. Also originally from the east coast, batik is now printed by factories all over the country, on fabrics ranging from cotton and voile to silk and satin. It is used for clothes, accessories, household and decorative items.

Pewterware

Silvercraft and Pewterware

Kelantan silvercraft comes in filigree, where ornamental wire is shaped into delicate tracery, or repousses, where sheet silver is hammered into patterned relief. Kelantan silver is fashioned into a variety of items, from brooches and costume jewellery to serving dishes and tableware.

KL's own local handicraft, Royal Selangor pewterware, enjoys a worldwide reputation for its stylish and attractive handmade designs. Pewter is an alloy of tin mixed with a little copper and antimony and was introduced to Malaysia from China in the 18th century. The hardness of the metal gives it durability, and its silvery finish does not tarnish. Products range from tableware and ornamental pieces to lapel pins, figurines and pendants.

Woven and Wooden Products

Cane and wicker are used for furniture and household items. Based on Malay and indigenous traditions, *mengkuang* (*pandanus*) leaves are woven into mats, baskets, hats and decorative items, and split bamboo strips are shaped into trays, baskets and household items.

Beadwork, native to Sabah and Sarawak, is extremely attractive when sewn onto headbands, necklaces, belts, buttons and baskets. Those available for sale in KL tend to be commercialised, but still make for attractive souvenirs.

Where to Buy

Handicrafts can be purchased from the **Kompleks Kraf Kuala Lumpur,** particularly during the International Craft Festival (see page 64), the **Central Market** (see page 37), **Peter Hoe Evolution**, **Beyond at The Row** (www.facebook.com/Peterhoecafe) and **Pucuk Rebung** (www.pucukrebung.com). Museum shops and flea markets are other good options. Pewter gifts and homeware can be purchased in department stores and from Royal Selangor boutiques in Setapak Jaya (my.royalselangor.com) and major malls. Wood veneer products are available at the KL Gallery (see page 35) and malls.

Ethnic Fashion

The delicate Peranakan *kebaya* best represents the fusion of cultures in Malaysia, having evolved since the 16th century with European and Chinese influences. Unlike the long and voluminous Malay-style *baju kurung*, the *kebaya* is hip-length, form-fitting and often made with semi-transparent materials such as voile, silk and muslin. Exquisitely embroidered front panels, often with floral designs, are characteristic. Worn on formal or festive occasions, both modern and traditional pieces are easily available. Other local traditional dress include the Chinese cheongsam and the Indian sari or *salwa khameez* trouser-suit. For men, there is the *baju Melayu*, a cotton or silk outfit with a mandarin collar and *sampin*, a sarong worn around the hips, and the Indian *khurta* cotton top.

Beaded shoes

Shopping for fabric

Meanwhile, **Jalan Masjid India** and **Jalan Tuanku Abdul Rahman** are good places to shop for traditional fabrics.

FASHION

Malaysia is a good and affordable place to purchase textiles and apparel of good-quality cotton, linen and silk. Most department stores carry selections of local and international brands. Outfits are usually best suited to warm, tropical climates, and tailors are equipped to handle alterations and made-to-measure orders at reasonable prices, sometimes delivering within 24 hours.

KL has all the international designer labels for the brand-conscious, but the truly great buys are Malaysian-designed fashion brands. **Vincci** (www.facebook.com/Vincci-1453849711514587) is a chain that does trendy, affordable women's shoes and accessories, while **Padini** (www.padini.com) carries both reasonably priced basics and seasonal discounts. **British India** (www.british india.com) is more upmarket, with ethnic home furnishings and well-designed clothes of natural fabrics for the whole family. Among couturiers, **Zang Toi Collection** (www.zangtoi.com) carries the lower-priced diffusion lines, **Khoon Hooi** (www.khoonhooi.com) mixes high fashion and street cred, **Salabianca** (www.salabianca.com.my) focuses on glamour while **Tom Abang Saufi** (www.tomabang saufi.com) crafts contemporary heritage-influenced haute couture.

ELECTRONICS AND IT PRODUCTS

Cameras, computers and IT equipment are relatively inexpensive in KL as they are duty free. A wide variety of these items is available, and retail outlets can be found in shopping malls. Dedicated IT malls are **Plaza Low Yat** in Bukit Bintang (see page 66) and the **Digital Mall** in Petaling Jaya (digitalmall.com.my/portal cms).

ART

Most contemporary art on view in the many commercial art galleries in the city and the Klang Valley are by home-grown artists. Although some have gained significant international exposure, the majority are emerging artists. In addition, exhibitions by regional artists are also staged. Check lifestyle guides for exhibition listings and visit the **National Visual Arts Gallery** (www.artgallery.gov.my) for a primer on who's who in Malaysian art. Among the leading galleries are **Hom Art Trans** (www.homarttrans.com), **Wei-Ling Gallery** (see page 55), **Gallery Chandan** (www.galerichandan.com), **Galeri Taksu** (www.taksu.com), **MAP** at **Publika** (www.facebook.com/mapkl) and **Richard Koh Fine Art** (www.rkfine art.com). Artists' collectives like **Lost-gens and Findars** (see page 40) and **Rumah Air Panas** (www.rap.twofishy. net) are working studio spaces as well as exhibition venues that run talks and alternative festivals.

Helipad Bar

ENTERTAINMENT

From the contemporary to the cultural, the sophisticated to the eclectic and the wild to the homely, KL offers something for everyone when it comes to having a good time.

An evening out in KL always starts with food and often ends with food too. In between, the diversions are many, including underground music gigs, fervent partying in trendy clubs or a classical Indian dance performance. See Nightlife listings on page 120. Weekends and the eve of pubic holidays offer great action but KL shifts into party overdrive during special occasions like New Year's Eve or when Formula 1 hits town. Then, the streets are closed to traffic, concerts are held and fireworks light up the sky. Popular venues for these events are the KLCC and Bukit Bintang. Meanwhile, concerts and music and arts festivals fill the calendar year-round: check online event listings.

CLUBS AND BARS

KL's clubbing scene is among the best in the region, with sophisticated venues, international DJs and a wide range of music choices. On weekends, the club scene rocks until dawn. Meanwhile, bars range from the super-swanky inner city rooftop outfits with views of the skyline, to friendly, backyard outfits in the suburbs. Specialist wine, whisky, gin and cigar bars are becoming increasingly popular. The nightlife areas are clustered at the massive **TREC** (www.trec.com.my) on Jalan Tun Razak and around KLCC and Changkat Bukit Bintang. Other venues include **KL Hilton**, **The Row** (www.therowkl.com).hotel at the Starhill Gallery end of Bukit Bintang, and **Bangsar**.

Stand-up comedy has a growing audience in KL. You can catch acts at some clubs and performance venues. The go-to place though, is the **Crackhouse Comedy Club** (www.facebook.com/crackhousecomedy) with good local and international talent.

Nightlife choices for the LGBT community are plentiful, if discrete. These include eateries, spas, saunas, cabarets and clubs such as the **Blue Boy Club** (www.facebook.com/pages/Blue-Boy-Club-Bukit-Bintang/197033543684106), the weekend **DivineBliss** @ Rooftop (www.view.com.my) and the **Market Place Lounge Bar** (www.mpkualalumpur.com/index.html). Straight clubs and bars are LGBT-friendly and also hold LGBT nights.

MUSIC

From DJs and bands to the classical and traditional, music is a vibrant part

Indian classical dance   *Jalan Bukit Bintang*

of life. Concerts begin at 8.30pm but sets in pubs and nightlife venues start late, usually around 10pm or 11pm, and there is normally a cover charge.

Club DJs spin everything from EDM to R&B and reggae; home-grown talents are budding while KL is firmly on the regional and international DJ circuit. In contrast, the entertainment in hotel lounges comprises easy listening music by a live band, usually Filipino, or a singer and pianist. Elsewhere, local bands mostly perform Billboard chart-toppers and dance numbers whilst the indie and underground music scene comprises a wide range of sub-genres including punk, experimental and post-grunge. Jazz has a loyal following in higher-end bars and venues. Karaoke is immensely popular and some outfits are plush, hi-tech and fun. The top classical concert venue is the **Dewan Filharmonik Petronas**, with a full programme by the Malaysian Philharmonic Orchestra and international musicians. Classical/traditional Indian and Chinese music concerts are staged by various cultural groups such as the **Temple of Fine Arts** (www.tfa.org. my) and **Dama Orchestra** (www.dama orchestra.com), respectively.

PERFORMING ARTS

There is a small but active theatre and dance scene in KL. Of note are innovative intercultural works that engage both Asian and Western forms to showcase traditional aspects of Malaysia life in startling and new ways. The main venues include the **Kuala Lumpur Performing Arts Centre**, **Damansara Performing Arts Centre**, **MAP** at **Publika** (www.facebook.com/mapkl) and the enormous **Istana Budaya** (National Theatre, www. istanabudaya.gov.my).

Traditional and cultural performances are staged at **Matic**, **the KL Tower** and **Central Market**. Of note are the excellent monthly **Pusaka** evenings held at **Publika**. **The Temple of Fine Arts and Sutra House** (www.sutrafoundation.org. my) stage notable classical Indian performances while Dama puts on good classical and period Chinese shows.

CINEMA

Cinemas are located in malls, have the latest technology and show the newest commercial releases largely from Hollywood but also Bollywood, Hong Kong/China, East Asia and South-east Asia. Local films are also popular. **Mid Valley Megamall** and **Pavilion** have international sections that screen art-house films. For independent films, the **Malaysian Film Club** (www.facebook.com/kelabsenifilemmalaysia) screens Malaysian and foreign films and student work. Screening independent films has also become trendy in bars and art spaces in **Changkat**, the **Petaling Street** vicinity and **MAP**. Film festivals are held regularly and among them, the **Freedom Film Fest** (www.freedomfilmfest.komas. org) is notable for its human rights focus.

National Day festivities

FESTIVALS

The city's multicultural society celebrates in colourful fashion all year-round, often spectacularly. Many festivals have a religious aspect to them, while all are familial and communal.

KL has a year-round calendar of traditional festivals. In public, the lead-up to major festivals sees different parts of the city and all shopping malls decked in the respective cultural decorations whilst selling festive goodies and clothing. During the festival, the religious will throng places of worship. Most will discard Western clothing for traditional outfits, often celebrating by visiting family and throwing 'open houses', inviting both family and friends home for meals and refreshments. Government-run 'open houses' are also held in public venues, and everyone is welcome. The three major festivals of **Hari Raya Aidilfitri**, **Chinese New Year** and **Deepavali** see a massive exodus out of KL and highways are packed before and after these holidays.

Fridays are important prayer days in mosques Sundays are sacred for many churches and temples. Buddhist/Taoist temples are busier on the first and 15th days of the lunar months; both these and Hindu temples also observe festivals related to their respective deities.

Muslim festivals are variable as they adhere to the Muslim calendar. Check **Tourism Malaysia** (www.malaysia.travel) for details.

January/February

Thaipusam: This festival of repentance sees Hindu worshippers gather on the eve at the Sri Maha Mariamman Temple. At dawn, a procession with a chariot carrying the deity Lord Murugan's statue makes its way to Batu Caves outside the city, the priests giving blessings at Hindu temples en route. At Batu Caves, devotees carry altars and pots of milk to the hilltop temple (see page 68).

Chinese New Year: Traditionally celebrated over 15 days, the run-up to the New Year is exciting at Petaling Street, with decorations and goodies galore from mandarin oranges to barbecued pork. On the eve, families gather for reunion meals, while the rest of the festival sees lion dances herald new beginnings and youngsters receive "red packets" – cash gifts from their elders for good luck.

March/April

Indian New Year: Mid-April marks the New Year for several communities, including Tamils, Punjabis and Malayalis – who throng Hindu temples for prayers – as well as Thais who celebrate with the wet Songkran Water Festival in Thai Buddhist temples.

Wesak Day   *Worshippers at Thaipusam*

May/June

Wesak Day: This day commemorates Buddha's birth, enlightenment and death. Devotees offer prayers and give alms to monks at Buddhist temples. Decorative float and candle processions begin and end at several major Buddhist temples such as the Maha Vihara Temple in Brickfields.

July/August

National Day (31 August): Malaysia celebrates its Independence Day with pomp and pageantry. Join the countdown and free open-air concert on the eve at Dataran Merdeka. The grand National Day parade, if hosted in Kuala Lumpur, is usually along Jalan Raja in front of Dataran Merdeka. Celebrations sometimes continue till Malaysia Day on 16 September, which commemorates the formation of Malaysia comprising the peninsula and the Borneon states.

September

Festival of the Hungry Ghosts: Chinese believe that during the seventh month of the lunar calendar, the gates of hell open and lost souls in purgatory roam the earth. Believers offer food, joss sticks and burn 'hell money' on pavements, while Chinese operas and concerts are staged to appease the spirits.

October/November

Deepavali: Hindus celebrate the triumph of good over evil in the seventh month of the Hindu calendar. They perform cleansing rituals and thanksgiving at home and in temples, and oil lamps are lit to receive blessings from Lakshmi, the goddess of wealth.

December

Christmas: Christians celebrate with carolling, nativity plays and cantatas and midnight masses on Christmas Eve. At home, they partake in gift-giving and family gatherings over meals, which could range from roast turkey to curry, while decorations include imitation fir trees and fake snow.

New Year's Eve: Countdowns are celebrated in different parts of the city with free concerts, fireworks and much merry-making. Restaurants also offer special menus, while clubbers across the city party until dawn.

Variable Dates

Hari Raya Puasa: The first day of the Muslim month of Shawal follows a month of fasting and prayers known as Ramadan. Ramadan is exciting for food bazaar throughout the city. Muslims usher in Hari Raya Aidilfitri by visiting ancestral graves and offering prayers, and seeking forgiveness from their elders, and celebrating with food.

Hari Raya Haji: This Muslim festival marking the *haj*, or religious pilgrimage to Mecca, is more solemn than Hari Raya Aidilfitri. Donated cows and sheep are slaughtered and their meat is distributed to the poor and needy at mosques.

A bronze etching, depicting Malaysian Independence Day in 1957

HISTORY: KEY DATES

Kuala Lumpur was a remote mining town that grew to become Malaysia's capital. Through colonisation, post-independence economic and social planning, and the 'can-do' era of the 1990s, the city has become a regional powerhouse.

EARLY HISTORY

AD 700–1400	The peninsula comes under the control of the Southeast Asian Hindu empire known as Srivijaya.
c.1400	The port and sultanate of Melaka, the first great maritime power on the peninsula, is founded. Islam, first brought by traders and missionaries, becomes the state religion in 1446.

THE BIRTH OF KUALA LUMPUR

1857	KL is founded by tin miners and becomes a staging point for the trading of tin. Chinese labour is imported.
1867	Selangor is torn by civil war over the imposition of export duties on tin ore. War spreads to KL; in 1872, the settlement is razed.
1868–85	Yap Ah Loy is KL's 'Kapitan Cina' and develops the town.

BRITISH MALAYA

1895	The Federated Malay States are formed.
1896	KL is declared capital of the Federated Malay States by the British.
1941–5	Japanese occupy the Malay Peninsula; British regain control after World War II.
1946	Rise of Malay nationalism. Local political parties become organised.
1948	The Federation of Malaya is created, bringing together all peninsular states under British rule. The guerilla insurgency by the Malayan Communist Party leads to a State of Emergency.
1955	Malaya's first national election; the Alliance of enthic-based political parties wins 80 percent of votes.
1957	31 August: Malaya becomes an independent nation, with Tunku Abdul Rahman as prime minister. KL is made the capital of Malaya.

Protestors demand the resignation of Malaysian Prime Minister Najib Razak in 2015

POST-INDEPENDENCE

1963	Singapore, Sabah and Sarawak join Malaya to form Malaysia.
1965	Singapore withdraws from Malaysia to become a republic.
1972	KL is accorded city status.
1974	KL is annexed from Selangor to become a Federal Territory.

TIGER ECONOMY

1988	The beginning of double-digit economic growth. Skyscrapers and mega-projects begin to transform KL's cityscape.
1991	The policy, Vision 2020, aims to make Malaysia a developed nation by 2020
1998	Asian Economic Crisis ends tiger economy growth, and currency controls are imposed. Reformasi (reformation) sees the start of strong political opposition.
1999	The Federal government's administrative offices move to Putrajaya; KL is now legislative capital, as well as financial and commercial centre.

REJUVENATION AND DEMOCRACY

2004	KL Structure Plan 2020, focusing on urban growth and development, is gazetted.
2007	Street demonstrations voice public dissatisfaction with the ruling party's administration and demand electoral reform.
2008	General elections result in historic loses by the ruling political coalition.
2009	Najib Razak replaces Abdullah Ahmad Badawi as prime minister.
2010	Multi-billion ringgit federal project sets a 10-year rejuvenation programme into motion, focusing on KL and the Klang Valley.
2012	Following Malaysia's largest-ever street demonstrations, the political opposition win popular vote but fail to win government.
2015	Malaysia's economy starts to slow down, due in part to the GST imposition and the minor global economic downturn. Protestors take to the streets and demonstrate against PM Najib Razak.
2016	KL is ranked as the world's 7th-most visited international travel destination by the Global Destinations Cities Index.

BEST ROUTES

Bangunan Sultan Abdul

HERITAGE QUARTER

Kuala Lumpur's original settlement began at the confluence of the Klang and Gombak rivers. Today, the centuries-old colonial buildings, minarets, spires and arches of the area are sights that bewitch.

DISTANCE: 3.5km (2.3 miles)
TIME: A full day
START: Medan Pasar Lama
END: Central Market
POINTS TO NOTE: Take the LRT to the Pasar Seni station, cross the road, walk past the Central Market until you reach a square with a clock tower. This is Medan Pasar Lama, the starting point.

This route first leads you around the colonial administrative centre, which has a cluster of graceful Mughal-style buildings encircling a town field. The walk then takes you through more contemporary surroundings to another pair of magnificent Mughal-style edifices owned by the National Railways. End the day at the Central Market, a cultural attraction and souvenir marketplace.

MEDAN PASAR LAMA

There is no signage that indicates the location of the **Medan Pasar Lama** ❶ (Old Market Square), as the original demarcations have disappeared due to urban renewal. Now roughly bordered by the streets of Lebuh Pasar Besar and Medan Pasar, what's left of the square was originally the business and social centre of KL's early mining settlement, with a bustling market, brothels, and gambling and opium dens, housed in buildings made of wood and attap. The wooden huts were destroyed in the great fire of 1881, and the city's first brick houses were then built to replace them, under the governance of British resident Frank Swettenham and local Chinese leader Yap Ah Loy. These were later demolished to make way for the double- and three-storey shophouses that now typify the architecture of the area.

Shophouses

These shophouses typically extend 30–60 metres to the back, with the ground floor used for business, usually a shop; upstairs was where the proprietor's family lived. The newer three-storey shophouses were built in 1906–7 and they incorporated Western decorative details like fluted pilasters and ornate

Medan Pasar Lama

Royal Selangor Club

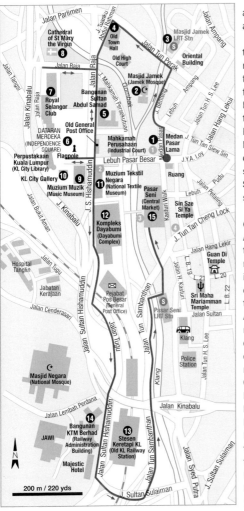

arched window frames and fanlights.

Today, only about half the shophouses have retained their original facades, each one different from its neighbour's. Housed in one of them on the left corner of Lebuh Pasar Besar and Medan Pasar is the traditional *kopitiam* (coffee shop) **Café Old Market Square**, (see ❶), a good spot for breakfast.

Clock Tower
After breakfast, walk to the **clock tower** in the middle of the square. This is one of several examples of 1920s–30s Art Deco that also dot central KL. A period piece with a signature sunburst motif, the clock was built in 1937 to commemorate the coronation of England's King George VI. Another fine Art Deco construction gently hugs the corner of Lebuh Pasar Besar and Jalan Hang Kasturi. Known as the OCBC building, after the bank for which it was built, this beauty now houses community space Ruang by Think City. A

Masjid Jamek

wonderful community-building initiative to bring people back into the city, Ruang hosts workshops, talks and exhibitions, often involving the neighbourhood; find out what's going on via their Facebook page.

JAMEK MOSQUE

Head north on the Medan Pasar square till you come to the river. A massive, lengthy makeover river-side is slowly changing the feel of this area to include tree-lined boulevards and cafés. On your left you can clearly see the confluence of the Gombak and Klang rivers. This site has been occupied since 1909 by the graceful **Masjid Jamek** ❷ (Jamek Mosque; tel: 03-22746063; Sat–Thu 8.30am–12.30pm; 2.30–4pm Fri 8.30–11am, 2.30–4pm), the city's oldest mosque, with a sprawl of colonnades and spires around a peaceful square. Designed by colonial architect A.B. Hubback, it was the first mosque in KL to have an onion-shaped dome. Recent renovations have uncovered historic steps leading down to the confluence, which Muslims used to access the river to perform their pre-prayer washing ritual.

Masjid Jamek LRT Station

Walk along the river towards the Masjid Jamek LRT station 3 until you reach Jalan Tun Perak. Across it, obscured by the LRT lines, is the **Oriental Building** ❸. This Art Deco style building, which was built in the 1930s, was designed to look like an antique radio as a reflection of the identity of its original owner, Radio Malaya. The best view of it is from the platform 2 of the LRT station, which is upstairs. Platform 1, on the opposite side, offers a great view of Masjid Jamek. The station also hosts an arts and culture event called Arts on the Move (www.thinkcity.com.my; Tue and Thu 5–7pm), which sees performances on the foyer facing Jalan Melaka and visual art on the 60 metre (200-ft) -long tunnel, which connects the two sides of the station beneath Jalan Tun Perak.

COLONIAL CORE

From the junction, turn left and walk past the LRT station along Jalan Tun

Musical at Panggung Bandaraya

Fountain on Jalan Raja

Panggung Bandaraya

Perak. This road leads to the city's colonial core, the most regal neighbourhood with Mughal-style public buildings. These were erected in the 1890s around the Dataran Merdeka (Independence Square) by the British administrators of the Federated Malay States (FMS). For some reason, the colonial architects of the Public Works Department deemed the Mughal style of architecture appropriate for the government buildings of the Malay Peninsula. Featuring domes, minarets and arches, this distinct style was imported from another British outpost, India. After independence, most of these edifices served as courts before eventually being taken over as offices.

Jalan Tun Perak

Walk along Jalan Tun Perak, skirting a long narrow building with a colonnade of clover-shaped arches on your left. Constructed in 1910, this was once the **FMS Survey Office**, from where public services were administered. The building hugs the corner of Jalan Tun Perak and Jalan Raja, which is where its entrance faces. Adjoining it is the **Old Town Hall ❹**, which, like the Survey Office, also sports a domed porch. It hosts the **Panggung Bandaraya** (City Hall Theatre), where the long-running exuberant musical about KL's origins, *Mud*, is a staple (tel: 03-26023335; www.mudKL.com). Behind the Town Hall, distinguished by pepper-pot turrets and double-columned arches, is the **Old High Court**.

Jalan Raja

The boulevard in front of these buildings is **Jalan Raja**. This road often hosts festive parades such as the cultural parade that kicks off the Citrawarna Malaysia (Colours of Malaysia) tourism event and occasional National Day parades on 31 August. For more information, see www.malaysia.travel.

Bangunan Sultan Abdul Samad

Walk across the bridge over the river and cross Jalan Raja at the pedestrian crossing to get to Dataran Merdeka. Once on the other side of the road, turn around for a good view of the magnificent **Bangunan Sultan Abdul Samad ❺** (Sultan Abdul Samad Building). The first Mughal-style building to be erected in the city, c.1897, it was once the colonial administrative centre, designed by colonial architects such as Arthur Charles Norman and R.A.J. Bidwell. Before it was built, KL had never had anything like it, a work of symmetry with colonnades and notched parapets anchored by a square clock tower, stretching 137m (450ft) along Jalan Raja. Named after the Sultan of Selangor at the time, the building took three years to complete. A factory was even specially set up in the suburbs to supply the millions of bricks required to build it. Come back again at night to see this resplendent work; it is a very pretty sight when lit up. At its southern end is a Tourist Information Centre (tel: 03-2602 2014; www.malaysia.travel; daily 9am–6pm).

INDEPENDENCE SQUARE

Turn to face **Dataran Merdeka ❻**. Once the British parade and cricket ground known as the Padang ('field' in Malay), this green was renamed after the country became a sovereign nation.

At the other side of the square is a cluster of Tudor-style buildings. This is another colonial relic, the members-only **Royal Selangor Club ❼**, built c.1884 and the nexus of British social life in the late 19th century. It still prides itself on an ambience that dates back to the days when Somerset Maugham was a regular visitor. The club houses the Long Bar, which has existed since club membership was restricted to male colonials. Today, the gender bias remains, hiding behind the excuse of tradition: women are still not allowed into the Long Bar; nor are they allowed to vote in club elections or hold positions on the board.

ST MARY'S CATHEDRAL

To the right used to be the Royal Selangor Club's stables, which were flattened to make way for the church that stands there now, the **Cathedral of St Mary the Virgin ❽** (tel: 03-2692 8672; www.stmaryscathedral.org.my; daily 8am–2pm). Consecrated in 1887, St Mary's is one of the region's oldest Anglican churches and served as the main place of worship for the British in the colonial period. The current structure was rebuilt in the English Gothic style in 1922 following a fire. To cater to its diverse congregation, it holds services in English, Malay, Iban and Nepali.

Victorian Fountain

Walk towards the southern end of Dataran Merdeka. You will pass an ornate **Victorian Fountain**. Some sources say it was brought from England to be placed at the Market Square, only to be moved to the field because the former site was too congested; others say it was built to honour a former British inspector of police.

Flagpole

The southern end of Dataran Merdeka is anchored by a **flagpole**, the tallest in Malaysia and one of the tallest in the world. It was here at midnight on 31 August 1957 that England's Union Jack was lowered for the last time – on the shorter flagpole that used to stand here – and Malaysia became an independent nation. Since then, the field has been the venue for the annual countdown to National Day. At the stroke of midnight, the big clock at Bangunan Sultan Abdul Samad strikes to herald 31 August, accompanied by much revelry and fireworks. On 31 December every year, large crowds also gather here to count down to the New Year.

Music Museum

Otherwise, continue walking to the end of Dataran Merdeka. Straight ahead, across

Dataran Merdeka

Lebuh Pasar, are two other historical buildings. At the corner is a three-storey Mughal-style structure, which originally served as the **Chartered Bank of India, Australia and China**, where the colonial government held its accounts. It is now a **Muzium Muzik** ❾ (Music Museum; tel: 03-2604 0176; www.jmm.gov.my/en/muzium-muzik; 9am–6pm; free), a tiny museum for enthusiasts of local musical instruments.

Kuala Lumpur City Gallery

Next to it is another period piece, the former **Government Printing Office**. A departure from the Mughal style, it has a no-frills Neo-Renaissance design that reflects its functional purpose. This is a popular selfie pit-stop for its giant 'I {heart} KL' sculpture. Inside is the **Kuala Lumpur City Gallery** ❿ (tel: 03-2698 3333; www.klcitygallery.com; 9am–6.30pm; free), which features a spectacular 12 x 15m scale model of KL. It also has a small history section and you can book free guided walking tours here, but it is mostly a showcase and gift shop for the wood veneer souvenir company Arch.

Next to it is the massive **Perpustakaan Kuala Lumpur** (Kuala Lumpur City Library; tel: 03-2692 6204; Mon 2–6.45pm, Tue–Fri 10am–6.45pm, Sat–Sun 10am–5pm; free), which sports large black domes, personifying architects' attempt to incorporate Mughal features into a more contemporary form. It has a good digitised collection of

materials about the city, including photographs, videos and news clippings.

Textile Museum

Head back to Jalan Raja and cross over to get to the orange-and-white **Muzium Tekstil Negara** ⓫ (National Textile Museum; tel: 03-2694 3457; www.muziumtekstil negara.gov.my; 9am–6pm; free). This was the colonial **FMS Railway Headquarters**, a striking building of ornamental rectangular columns and bricks. Displays at the museum include historical textiles and ornaments of different ethnic groups. Have a drink or a meal at its charming gem of a **café** (see ➋).

DAYABUMI COMPLEX

It's now a 750-metre walk to the next attraction. Walk south along what is now Jalan Sultan Hishamuddin, towards the gleaming white **Kompleks Dayabumi** ⓬ (Dayabumi Complex), with fine filigree-like Islamic design. This is KL's first steel-frame skyscraper, which was completed in 1984, and marked the start of a trend of buildings with a local Islamic identity. The intricate design also doubles as a sun shade. The building is at its most impressive at night, when it is floodlit. Go past the **General Post Office** (tel: 1300-300 300; Mon–Fri 8.30am–6pm; Sat 8.30am–1pm) and keep left. You'll be able to see the blue roof of the National Mosque on the other side of the road. Keep going until you hit the

Bangunan KTM Berhad

roundabout. Ahead are the last of the Mughal-style buildings that were constructed during the colonial era.

RAILWAY BUILDINGS

The structure before you is the **Stesen Keretapi Kuala Lumpur** ⑬ (Old KL Railway Station). It faces the **Bangunan KTM Berhad** ⑭ (Railway Administration Building). Both are stunning pieces of architecture with a pastiche of various elements such as Mughal minarets, Gothic windows and Greek columns. Designed by the same architect as the Masjid Jamek, A.B. Hubback, the latter continues to house the offices of the Malaysian Railways, but the Old KL Railway Station has been underused since the interstate rail services were moved to the modern KL Sentral transport hub.

Now, only ktm Komuter trains depart from the centre platform to Port Klang, Seremban and Rawang. The Nice Bus Company also operates services to Penang and Singapore from here. Go round the railway station to get to Jalan Tun Sambanthan. As you leave the station, note the white building across the road. This is the Majestic Hotel, in colonial times the pre-eminent place to stay and the centre for glamorous high-society soirees. The neoclassical/ Art Deco facade has been restored and it is now once again a luxury hotel, together with a modern, adjacent wing (see page 103).

As you cross the bridge, note the height of the railway station's roof; a building specification by the British colonialists was that the station's roof be able to hold 1 metre (3ft) of snow, a somewhat curious requirement for a building in the tropics.

CENTRAL MARKET

At Jalan Tun Sambanthan, turn left and walk about 100 metres along the station until you see an overhead pedestrian walkway. Go up it and turn right to

---

River of Life

Shady greenery, bicycle lanes and cafés galore will be some of the features of this quarter's waterfront after a huge makeover. This is the first phase of the RM1 billion River of Life Project, covering 110 km (68 miles) of waterways within the city and further afield. Scheduled for a 2020 completion date, it aims to raise the river quality, develop the riverbanks and improve the capacity for recreational activities in the area. A major issue has been the relocating of squatters and illegal factories upstream. To bring people back to this part of the city, urban rejuvenation projects are being carried out. Government agency Think City is engaging property and business owners, residents and NGOs in a 1-km (.75 mile) -radius around Masjid Jamek, in community-building, renewing old buildings and enlivening public spaces.

T-shirts at Central Market

Kasturi Walk

walk another 100 metres over the Klang River towards the Pasar Seni LRT station. From there, head to the **Central Market** ⑮ (Pasar Seni; tel: 03-2031 5399; www.centralmarket.com.my; daily 10am–10pm). Once the city's largest fresh produce market, the Central Market was converted into a cultural shopping mall during the late 1980s, with preserved Art Deco features and a high ceiling. This is an excellent place to shop for souvenirs, including handicrafts, clothes, antiques and art, all at fairly reasonable prices. Don't forget to bargain though!

Along the side of the Central Market is the Kasturi Walk, a pedestrian mall adorned with outsized *wau* (kites), where you can buy more souvenirs and snacks. Every Saturday from 6–9.30pm, it hosts cultural performance, buskers and food trucks. The mall's **annexe** focuses on artwork, including DIY batik and artists who can draw caricatures and portraits on the spot.

For great Asian food, head to **Restaurant Ginger** (see ③) or for simpler fare, try **Restoran Yusoof dan Zakir** (see ④), just outside the mall.

Food and Drink

① CAFÉ OLD MARKET SQUARE

2 Medan Pasar; http://cafeoldmarket square.com; Mon–Fri 7am–6pm, Sat 7am–3pm; $
This restored 80-year-old Hainanese coffee shop serves a favourite local breakfast. Start your day with toast and *kaya* (coconut and egg jam), a soft-boiled egg and a strong coffee.

② THE CANTEEN BY CHEF ADU

Muzium Tekstil Negara, 26 Jalan Sultan Hishamuddin; tel: 03-2694 3457; daily 9am–6pm; www.facebook. com/The-Canteen-by-Chef-Adu-1032245193507769; $$
This cosy and charming celebrity chef-run eatery serves the best food from the southern state of Johor. Must-tries are the

Laksa Johor spicy sour noodle soup and the cottage pie with a local twist. Credit cards not accepted.

③ RESTAURANT GINGER

Lot M12, Central Market; tel: 03-2273 7371; daily 11.30am–9.30pm; $$
Order the spicy Malay *rendang* (dry beef or chicken curry), Thai green chicken curry and Indonesian fried rice accompanied by *satay* at this sumptuously decorated restaurant.

④ RESTORAN YUSOOF DAN ZAKIR

44 & 46 Jalan Hang Kasturi; tel: 03-2026 8685; daily 24 hours; $
A fan-cooled no frills eatery, abuzz with locals who come for the good variety of Indian *roti* (breads) and north Indian curries. Service is quick – your *roti* arrives within minutes of ordering.

Petaling Street bazaar

PETALING STREET

A tourist magnet and a bargain hunter's paradise most famous for its street bazaar, Petaling Street also offers plenty of eateries, temples and clanhouses, many of which have survived from the time of the city's beginnings.

DISTANCE: 3km (1¾ miles)
TIME: A full day
START: Petaling Street Gateway
END: Sin Sze Si Ya Temple
POINTS TO NOTE: From the Pasar Seni lrt station, turn right onto Jalan Tun Tan Cheng Lock and walk about 500 metres to the junction of Jalan Petaling and Jalan Tun Tan Cheng Lock.

The city's most famous street bazaar is often just referred to by the name of the main road it occupies: Petaling Street (Jalan Petaling). It sits in a bustling part of KL, dominated by pre-war Chinese-style shophouses. Although largely Chinese in character, the area also bears influences from other ethnic groups.

PETALING STREET MARKET

From the **Petaling Street gateway**, walk down Jalan Petaling, turn right onto Jalan Hang Lekir and look out for an entrance next to Hotel Malaya. This leads to the **Petaling Street Market ❶**

(daily 7am–3pm). Go early to experience the action and smells in this small, century-old fresh-produce market with vegetables, seafood, poultry and more.

PETALING STREET BAZAAR

Head back onto Jalan Petaling. On the left corner is a famous stall selling the *mata kucing* herbal drink (see ❶). You are now in KL's famous **Petaling Street Bazaar ❷** (daily 10am–11pm; free), which stretches along the stretch of Jalan Petaling and is bookended by gateways and the perpendicular Jalan Hang Lekir. The stalls offer mainly knock-offs of branded goods – bargain hard if you want to buy something or shop around, as you can usually find the same products at numerous stalls. There are also souvenirs, fruits and snacks, as well as some of best Chinese street food to be had in KL.

Petaling Street and its surroundings make for a calmer browse in the daytime. When the fluorescent lights come on, the atmosphere too becomes electric as the crowd and the sense of cut-throat commerce intensifies. If it gets

Sunglasses at the bazaar   *Sin Sze Si Ya Temple*

too much, leave the bustle and head to Jalan Sultan, a relatively quieter street of Chinese tea shops, traditional businesses and old-style eateries like **Seng Kee Restaurant** (see ❷).

CHAN SHE SHU YUEN

From Jalan Petaling, head south until you hit Jalan Stadium; at the corner sits the **Chan She Shu Yuen Association** ❸

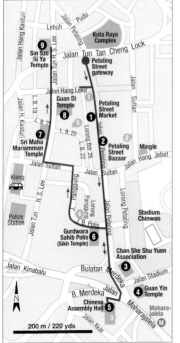

(tel: 03-2078 1461; daily 8am–5pm; free). This clan association has been looking after the needs of Chinese people with the surnames Chan, Chen and Tan since 1896. Note its roof, famously decorated with intricate ceramic figurines and wall friezes depicting Chinese mythology and history.

GUAN YIN TEMPLE

Across Jalan Stadium from the Chan She Shu Yuen Association is the delightful **Guan Yin Temple** ❹ (tel: 03-2070 8650; daily 8am–5pm), located at the top of a flight of steps guarded by a pair of stone lions. This century-old Hokkien temple has an image of a thousand-armed and thousand-eyed Guan Yin, the Goddess of Mercy. This is one of the few Hokkien temples in town, with a curved roof typical of such temples.

CHINESE ASSEMBLY HALL

Clan associations later became the Associated Chinese Chambers of Commerce. The national headquarters of the chambers was once located opposite the Chan She Shu Yuen Association. This is now the **Chinese Assembly Hall** ❺, housed in a white colonial-era building capped by a dome. Cross the overhead pedestrian bridge over Jalan Maharajalela to get to the hall. The left corner of the building is taken up by the **Purple Cane Cultural Centre**, an excellent choice for lunch (see ❸).

Breakfast in Chinatown

JALAN BALAI POLIS

After lunch, return to Jalan Petaling and turn left onto Jalan Balai Polis. On your left is the Sikh house of worship, the **Gurdwara Sahib Polis** ❻ (daily 9am–5pm; free). Sikhs were originally brought from India to the Malay states by the British to staff the police force and once made up its majority. A simple structure wearing the blue of Malaysian police buildings, it houses the *Guru Granth Sahib*, the Sikh holy book.

Clan associations

Chinese clan associations were established in the 19th century in KL to serve Chinese migrants who came to work in the mines. The largest groups were the Cantonese, Hakka and Hainanese. Clan houses (*kongsi*) provided accommodation, financial help and education. Key services were funeral services and the repatriation of bodies back to China. During World War II, these associations raised crucial funds to help China fight the Japanese. Most associations have patron deities to whom temples are built. Patron deity days and foundation days are observed. Over time, ties among association members grew into business networks and became the basis of commercial success. Many associations are now defunct but the *kongsi* remain interesting historical repositories.

Opposite the Sikh temple is the **Old China Café** (see ❹), serving Nonya (Peranakan) food and a potential spot for dinner. Behind its swinging doors, black-and-white photos and heavy marble-topped tables add to its delightful old-world atmosphere. From Jalan Balai Polis, turn right onto Jalan Panggung.

SRI MAHA MARIAMMAN TEMPLE

Turn left onto Jalan Sultan and right again onto Jalan Tun H.S. Lee. Named after a politician who was instrumental in helping Malaya gain independence from the British, Jalan Tun H.S. Lee is lined with elaborate 19th-century shophouses. It used to be called High Street because it was higher than the surrounding streets and therefore not as prone to flooding.

About 50 metres along Jalan Tun H.S. Lee is a gateway tower adorned with statues of Hindu deities. This is the entrance to the **Sri Maha Mariamman Temple** ❼ (tel: 03-2078 3467; daily 6am–1am). Dedicated to the Mother Goddess Mariamman, the temple is laid out in the shape of the human body. The gateway represents the feet, marking the threshold between the material and the spiritual worlds. Built in 1873, the temple occupies an important place in Hindu religious life.

GUAN DI TEMPLE

Diagonally opposite the Hindu temple in an obscure lane is a row of hawker stalls. If you are there between 11am and

Sri Maha Mariamman Temple

3pm and don't mind the no-frills environment, try out one of the best Hakka *yong tau foo* (see 5) in town. Otherwise, head next door to the **Guan Di Temple** ❽ (daily 7am–5pm; free). This fei Cantonese temple honours the red-faced Guan Di, the God of War and Literature, and the Tiger God, who is worshipped during the Lunar New Year to ward off troublemakers.

SIN SZE SI YA TEMPLE

Continue along Jalan Tun H.S. Lee. Cross Jalan Tun Tan Cheng Lock and then enter a discreet doorway, which is adorned with dragons, on the left. The doorway leads to the Taoist **Sin Sze Si Ya Temple** ❾ (tel: 03-2072 9593; daily 7am–5pm).

Constructed according to feng shui principles, you'll notice that the temple entrance oddly faces a corner. It was built by the Chinese leader Yap Ah Loy in 1864 to honour two of his comrades, Sin Sze Ya and Si Sze Ya. Their altars are in the main hall. After his death in 1885, Yap was also enshrined in the temple.

Food and Drink

❶ MATA KUCING DRINK STALL

Corner of Jalan Hang Lekir and Jalan Petaling; daily 10am–10pm; $
Serving the cooling local drink *mata kucing* (literally 'cat's eye'), made with three Asian fruits, including *longan*.

❷ SENG KEE RESTAURANT

52 Jalan Sultan; tel: 03-2072 5950; daily 11am–3am; $
Try its excellent Chinese-style noodles, such as the KL speciality Hokkien *mee* (noodles stir-fried in dark soy sauce) and claypot *loh shu fun* (rice noodles in a minced-pork sauce).

❸ PURPLE CANE

1 Jalan Maharajalela; tel: 03-2272 3090; www.purplecane.com.my; daily 11am–10pm; $

This serves 'tea cuisine' prepared with premium Chinese tea leaves. Try the simmered black-tea chicken with tea rice and the mushroom chicken cooked in *pu'er* tea.

❹ OLD CHINA CAFÉ

11 Jalan Balai Polis; tel: 03-2072 5915; www.oldchina.com.my; daily 11.30am–9.45pm; $$
The charming setting is the perfect place to sample Nonya specialities such as *ayam pongteh* (chicken stew) and *asam* prawns (tamarind prawns).

❺ MADRAS LANE HAKKA YONG TAU FOO

Lorong Bandar 20; Tue–Sun 11am–3pm; $
This famous hawker stall has been serving *yong tau foo* for 40 years. Choose from tofu, ladies fingers, chilli and other vegetables that are stuffed with fish paste, and have them in a soup or with a bean paste sauce.

KL Tower restaurant

KUALA LUMPUR CITY CENTRE

This route around KL's business district focuses on the Petronas Twin Towers and Menara Kuala Lumpur, both of which afford fabulous views. Their surroundings entice with nature, shopping and nightlife.

DISTANCE: 3.5km (2 1/3 miles)
TIME: A full day
START: Petronas Twin Towers
END: Menara Kuala Lumpur
POINTS TO NOTE: Take the LRT to the underground KLCC lrt station, which is linked to the Suria KLCC mall at the base of the Petronas Twin Towers. Aim to end the tour in the evening; the area offers numerous nightlife options.

KL feels very different in the day and to what it does at night-time, and a good way to take this in is from above, visiting one tower during the day and the other at dusk. The more iconic of the two, the Petronas Twin Towers, are part of the 40-ha (100-acre) **Kuala Lumpur City Centre** (KLCC), the focal point of a country charging towards developed-nation status. klcc comprises offices, which are housed in the gleaming Petronas Twin Towers and the surrounding skyscrapers, the Suria klcc shopping mall, a beautiful landscaped park, convention centre, aquarium and several luxury hotels.

PETRONAS TWIN TOWERS

The **Petronas Twin Towers ❶**, soaring 452 metres (1,483ft) into the sky, were the world's tallest buildings from 1996 to 2003. Now, as proud Malaysians are keen to point out, the towers remain the world's tallest *pair* of buildings.

KL Tower

Suria KLCC

Petronas Twin Towers

Named after and owned by the national petroleum company, the towers were designed by the renowned US-based architect Cesar Pelli and were built using 65,000 sq m (700,000 sq ft) of stainless-steel cladding, 160,000 cubic m (5.7 million cubic ft) of concrete and 77,000 sq m (830,000 sq ft) of glass. To express a Malaysian identity, the floor plans of the towers take after an eight-point star formed from two interlocking squares, a popular Islamic architectural motif, while the number of storeys – 88 – translates as 'double luck' in Chinese.

Good views of the Twin Towers can be had from the adjoining KLCC Park, though photography angles are bet-ter from Jalan Ampang and Jalan Tun Razak, as well as from the upper floors of various hotels in the area.

Observation deck

A bird's eye-view of KL can be enjoyed from the top of Tower 2 (tel: 03-2331 8080; 8080; www.petronastwintowers. com.my; Tue–Sun 9am–9pm, Fri closed 1–2.30pm; queue for tickets at the con-course of Tower 2 or book online). Eleva-tor doors open first for a 10-minute taster at the double-decker skybridge, which links the two towers on levels 41 and 42. You then go up to the level 86 observa-tion deck, where you have 20 minutes to take in Tower 1, the Menara Kuala Lum-

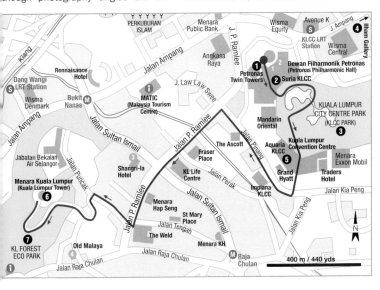

pur (see page 45) and the Greater KL sprawl up to the distant mountains

SURIA KLCC

At the base of the towers sits **Suria KLCC ❷** (tel: 03-2382 2828; www.suria kcc.com.my; daily 10am–10pm), a spacious, classy shopping mall with department stores and over 270 speciality shops. Anchored by three department stores Parkson (local), Isetan (Japanese) and Marks & Spencer (UK), it also has international and local designer and consumer brands. Bring your passport to get a tourist card for discounts at selected stores.

Science Museum and
Art Gallery

Children can easily spend hours at **Petrosains** (tel: 03-2331 8181; www. petrosains.com.my; Tue–Fri 9.30am–5.30pm, Sat–Sun 9.30am–6.30pm), on Level 6 of Suria KLCC. This is an excellent interactive museum on the oil and gas industry for families, run by Petronas. The national petroleum company also owns the elegant art gallery **Galeri Petronas** (Petronas Gallery; tel: 03-2051 7770; www.galeripetronas.com; Tue–Sun 10am–8pm; free) on Level 3. Contemporary and traditional works are exhibited here. On the ground level is the city's premier classical music venue, the **Dewan Filharmonik Petronas** (box office tel: 03-2051 7007; Tue–Sat 10.30am–6.30pm, Sun noon–perfor-

mance time and till 9pm on performance nights; dress code applies).

There are numerous eateries and food courts in Suria KLCC. For meals with a view, check out the brasserie **Chinoz on the Park** (see ❶) and the **Signatures Food Court** (see ❷), both overlooking the park.

KLCC PARK

Once the day cools down a little, head out to the **Suria Esplanade** to explore the **KLCC Park ❸**. The 'dancing' fountains on the lake fronting the Esplanade are a favourite with locals with 150 variations. Beyond the lake is a 20-ha (50-acre) artfully laid-out garden designed by the late Brazilian landscape artist Roberto Burle Marx. A jogging track winds around the lake, past fountains, sculptures and vegetation. The trees and shrubs in the park comprise of mainly indigenous species. About 40 trees were kept intact during the construction of KLCC and date back decades to the time when the area was the Selangor Turf Club. Children will enjoy the playground and wading pool (daily 10am–6pm; free).

Ilham Gallery

Art lovers might want to take a small diversion here to check out the beautiful **Ilham Gallery ❹** (www.facebook.com/ ilhamgallerykl; Tue–Sun 11am–7pm; free), 1km/ .5 mile to the east on Jalan Binjai via Jalan Ampang. A private-

Aquaria KLCC

ly-funded public art gallery, it holds critical, challenging themed shows with a strong public education purpose, and has diverse programmes that range from film screenings to performances and talks. Check out its outdoor Ai Weiwei sculptures and Pinaree Sanpitak's stupa topiary.

Convention Centre and Aquarium

Otherwise, head towards the **Kuala Lumpur Convention Centre**, a high-tech space for trade shows and conventions, where concerts and theatre performances are sometimes staged. Its concourse level is occupied by the **Aquaria KLCC** ❺ (tel: 03-2333 1888; www.klaquaria. com; daily 10am–8pm), a family-friendly interactive rainforest exhibition space and aquarium with more than 5,000 fish and other marine creatures. The submerged tunnel and moving walkway is a particular highlight.

KUALA LUMPUR TOWER

Head to the **Menara Kuala Lumpur** (more commonly known as the KL Tower) if you want a bird's-eye view of the city and the Petronas Twin Towers. To get there from Aquaria KLCC, exit onto Jalan Pinang and turn right. Walk along the road and turn left past a lovely park onto Jalan P. Ramlee. The road is named after a late Malaysian entertainment icon. His songs and movies, produced mainly in the 1950s and 1960s, are well-loved classics that continue to influence contemporary entertainers (there's a small section on him in the Music Museum, see page 35). Cross the Jalan Sultan Ismail junction. The Shangri-La hotel is on your right. Its **Lemon Garden 2Go** café (see ❸), serves delicious pastries. If you don't fancy stopping for tea, continue up the slope and turn onto Jalan Puncak on your right. On the left is the entrance to the KL Tower. You can walk uphill or take the free shuttle.

Tower Architecture

The tower head of the 421 metre (138-ft) -tall **KL Tower** ❻ (tel: 03-2020 5444; www.menarakl.com.my; daily 9am–10pm; book online to avoid queues) is inspired by the Malaysian *gasing*, a top that is used in a traditional game, and

Petronas Philharmonic Hall

KL Tower observation deck

the tower's design reflect an influence of Islamic motifs. Of note are the arches of the entrance lobby, which are adorned with glass that resembles diamonds. A super-swift lift delivers you up to the **observation deck** where you can get a 360-degree view of the city. The view of the Petronas Twin Towers is always a favourite selfie background, and if those towers appear shorter than where you are standing, they actually are because the Menara KL sits on top of a hill. Pay more to access the higher, open-air Sky Deck and transparent Sky Box (minimum age 13 years old); be warned though, it's not for the faint-hearted!

The building also has souvenir shops, cafés and a revolving restaurant. **Cultural shows** (Wed–Sun 9.30am–11am; free) are held at the amphitheatre.

BUKIT NANAS FOREST RESERVE

The KL Tower sits within the **Bukit Nanas Forest Reserve ❼** (tel: 03-2070 6342; daily 9am–5pm; free), the country's oldest forest reserve, gazetted in 1906. Bukit Nanas is the only remaining green lung in the brick-and-mortar clutter of the Golden Triangle. If there is still

MATIC

Bukit Nanas

light after you have visited the Menara Kuala Lumpur and you have comfortable shoes on, you might want to explore the forest, called the **Taman Eko Rimba KL** (KL Forest Eco Park).

It has a terrific 200-metre-long canopy walkway and four short, well-marked trails that wind through the shady rainforest, which is rich with insects, monkeys, birds and primary forest plant species. Be sure to wear insect repellent before you enter the forest. You can follow the trail all the way down to the **Forest Information Centre** on Jalan Raja Chulan. Around the centre, there are is herb garden and orchid house.

NIGHT UNDER THE TOWERS

If you end up at Jalan Raja Chulan, head west for 300 metres until you come to **Old Malaya** at No 66 (www.facebook.com/oldmalaya), a rambling 1919 building lot that was once the quarters of the Eurasian community. It has been renovated and turned into a restaurant hub. Enjoy great views of the floodlit KL Tower from the restaurants' downstairs and upstairs patios. Cool down with a 5–8pm happy hour beer or mojito at the outdoor **Bar 1919** or the indoor long bar at the **Kapitan Bar** (see ④).

Otherwise, return to Suria KLCC, where you can dine at one of its many eateries. After dinner, chill out at the Suria Esplanade and enjoy the lights of the Petronas Twin Towers, together with the colourful 'dancing' fountains.

Food and Drink

① CHINOZ ON THE PARK

Lot G47, G/F, Suria KLCC; tel: 03-2166 8277; daily 8.30am–10pm; $$

Great alfresco dining, overlooking the KLCC Park. The Mediterranean menu includes grilled fish, pastas, pizzas and sandwiches (try their signature burger). Always busy.

② SIGNATURES FOOD COURT

2/F, Suria KLCC; tel: 03-2382 2828; daily 10am–10pm; $–$$

This popular 28-outlet food court offers a good variety, from pasta to tandoori dishes and ice-cream to Thai desserts. Local and regional favourites include Ipoh noodles, Thai green curry and Japanese *teppanyaki*.

③ LEMON GARDEN 2GO

Lobby Level, Shangri-La Hotel; tel: 03-2074 3546; Mon–Fri 8am–6.30pm, Sat 9am–5pm; $$

This friendly deli serves great toasties and freshly baked pastries and cakes to go with good coffee. Malaysian options are available too.

④ BAR 19 & KAPITAN BAR

Old Malaya, 66 Jalan Raja Chulan; tel: 010-2533 381; daily 5pm–12am; $$

Part of the Pampas restaurant assemblage, Bar 19 has a beer garden with a colonial backdrop while the chic glass-ceilinged Kapitan Bar has a quirky birdcage-and-portrait deco.

The Butterfly Park

BOTANICAL GARDEN

A haven of landscaped greenery in the city, the Perdana Botanical Garden's numerous parks and museums can easily occupy a full day. The southern end is anchored by an excellent Islamic museum.

DISTANCE: 5km (3 miles)
TIME: A full day
START: Tugu Kebangsaan
END: Islamic Arts Museum
POINTS TO NOTE: Take a taxi to Tugu Kebangsaan. The Kuala Lumpur Hop-on Hop-off bus (see page 131) also stops at the entrance of the Botanical Garden; cross the road to get to the monument. Start the day early and enjoy the gardens in cooler weather.

Alfred Venning, the former British State Treasurer, was more interested in creating a paradisiacal botanical garden amid lakes in the heart of KL than he was in economics. Now, over 120 years later, the name Venning scarcely means anything to KL-ites, but his legacy lives on in the heart of the city.

PERDANA BOTANICAL GARDEN

Formerly known as the Lake Gardens, the **Perdana Botanical Garden** (Taman Botani Perdana; www.klbotanicalgarden.gov.my; daily 6am–8pm; free), with 104ha (257 acres) of close-cropped lawns, undulating hills and cultivated gardens, is a sanctuary from the maddening mayhem of the city. The leafy gardens are also a valuable green lung, helping to cleanse the city of its polluted air.

The Botanical Garden is popular with exercise enthusiasts, from joggers to t'ai chi practitioners, from dawn until dusk. Families throng the area on weekends, with picnic baskets in hand.

Besides plant collections, the garden's attractions include a bird park, with one of the region's largest aviaries; a butterfly park, a sanctuary for over 6,000 butterflies and moths; and an orchid garden with hundreds of luxuriant blooms.

You will not have time to visit all the attractions, so plan ahead (the website has a map). To avoid too much walking in the hot and humid weather, hire a taxi for a few hours and have it wait for you at the various attractions. The Kuala Lumpur Hop-on Hop-off service (see page 131) also goes through the gar-

National Monument

ASEAN Sculpture Garden

den. Pack a meal to enjoy in the park's many picnic areas.

National Monument

Start your tour at the **Tugu Negara** ❶ (National Monument), which commemorates local and foreign servicemen who died during the Communist insurgency of 1948–60. It was modelled after the Iwo Jima memorial in the United States. Steps lead down to a **cenotaph** commemorating the soldiers who died in the two World Wars.

ASEAN Sculpture Garden

Walk down the hill and through the **ASEAN Sculpture Garden** ❷ (free).

The sculptures are symbols of the alliance among the 10 nations of the Association of Southeast Asian Nations, of which Malaysia is a member.

BUTTERFLY PARK

Cross Jalan Parlimen and walk along Jalan Cenderawasih to get to the Botanical Garden. If you haven't had breakfast, pop into the multi-storey carpark on your left for a Malay breakfast at **Restoran Rebung Chef Ismail** (see ❶) on the 5th floor. From here, cross into the park's main entrance. On your right is the delightful Kia Klemenz souvenir shop (tel: 03-2276 6053; www.kiaklemenz.

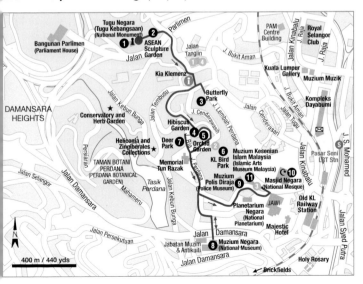

Kuala Lumpur Bird Park

com; Mon–Fri 9.30am–6.30pm, Sat–Sun 8.30am–7.30pm) where you can get park information and pastries and good coffee. At the end of the paved walkway, walk on for 300 metres and turn left into Jalan Tembusu and then walk 400 metres to the **Butterfly Park** ❸ (tel: 03-2693 4799; daily 9am–6pm), on Jalan Cenderasari. This pretty garden has thousands of plants that help re-create the butterflies' natural habitat. One of its buildings houses a collection of Malaysia's rainforest insects, reptiles and amphibians.

HIBISCUS PARK

Head back to Jalan Tembusu. Keep walking straight and the road becomes Jalan Cenderawasih. To the left is the **Hibiscus Gar** ❹. It has 2,500 hibiscus plants of different varieties from all over the world. Malaysian forests are home to several species of hibiscus, but, for some reason, the species that was chosen as Malaysia's national flower *(bunga raya)* is not actually native to the country but originates from Hawaii.

ORCHID GARDEN

A footpath at the back leads to the **Orchid Garden** ❺. There are about 2,000 orchid species in Malaysia. About 800-odd are grown in the Orchid Garden, home to a mix of both cultivated and wild orchids, and the colourful blooms are always a hit with visitors.

BIRD PARK

Take the main exit from the Orchid Garden and you will once again be on Jalan Cenderawasih. Across the road is the **Kuala Lumpur Bird Park** ❻ (tel: 03-2272 1010; www.klbirdpark.com; daily 9am–6pm). This 8-ha (20-acre) covered aviary is home to 3,000 birds of over 200 species. Except for a few free-flying species, most are housed in display and confined areas. Time your visit with feeding times and the bird show. Of note is the hornbill section, where you get close-up views of these large black-and-white creatures with prominent beaks and magnificent tails. Malaysia has 10 species of hornbills, some of which figure in the rites and beliefs of certain indigenous people. An excellent place to view them is the **Hornbill Restaurant & Café** (see ❷), located within the hornbill section where you can cool down with a drink or have lunch.

DEER PARK

From the Bird Park, turn left onto Jalan Cenderawasih and walk on until you reach the T-junction. Turn right onto Jalan Ria to get to the **Deer Park** ❼ (Mon–Thu 10am–noon and 2–6pm, Fri 10am–noon and 3–6pm, Sat–Sun 10am–6pm; free), which will appeal to children. The highlight here is the shy Mouse deer, the smallest deer in the world; it's about the size of a cat. The park has been successfully breeding

Hibiscus Park

Exhibition at the National Museum

these animals. Visitors can also feed Mauritian and Dutch deer.

ANCIENT OBSERVATORIES

Head back to the top of Jalan Ria. It becomes Jalan Perdana and passes the **Tun Razak Memorial**, which honours Malaysia's second prime minister and the current prime minister's father. After about 250 metres, you'll reach the mosque-like **Planetarium Negara** (National Planetarium). The building itself is not very interesting but its garden is dotted with replicas of ancient observatories, which are fun to try and figure out. Among them is the more recent Merdeka Sundial, built to commemorate Malaysian independence.

NATIONAL MUSEUM

A pedestrian bridge behind the planetarium leads to the back of the **Muzium Negara** ❽ (National Museum; tel: 03-2267 1000; www.muziumnegara. gov.my; daily 9am–6pm). The museum's exhibits are uninspiring but its architecture is outstanding. This is the first post-independence building designed in the neo-traditional instead of the Modernist style, reflecting the national identity of a new sovereign country. Its roofs are inspired by traditional Malay roofs and, perched on 26 pillars, the building is laid out like a Malay palace. Two massive batik murals depict the highlights of Malaysian history and culture.

POLICE MUSEUM

If you are keen to visit more museums, head back to the planetarium and onto Jalan Perdana to get to the **Muzium Polis Diraja Malaysia** ❾ (Royal Malaysian Police Museum; tel: 03-2272 5689; Tue–Sun 10am–6pm; free). It is a gem full of exhibits and audio visual material detailing the history of the police force from colonial times. The weapons section is among the most popular with visitors, featuring among others, guns from post-World War II China-aligned Communist guerrillas.

Planetarium Negara

National Mosque

NATIONAL MOSQUE

From the Police Museum, continue down Jalan Perdana for 400 metres until you hit Jalan Lembah Perdana. Ahead is the **Masjid Negara** ❿ (National Mosque; www.masjidnegara.gov.my/v2; Mon–Thu 9am–noon, 3–4pm, 5.30–6.30pm, Fri 3–4pm, 5.30–6.30pm), a sprawling mosque that is resplendent in white marble offset by pools of gurgling water. Completed in 1965, it was the first mosque to depart from the Mughal style of architecture and remains an icon of Modernism in Malaysian architecture.

The mosque's circular, ridged blue roof symbolises an open umbrella, while its 73 metre (240-ft) -tall minaret represents a closed umbrella. This motif is said to echo the pyramidal roof form of traditional Malay houses and its 16 spokes represent the nation's 13 states (although it is unclear what the additional three spokes stand for).

ISLAMIC ARTS MUSEUM

From here, continue along Jalan Lembah Pantai to the **Muzium Kesenian Islam**

> ## Bangsar
>
> The nearby neighbourhood of **Bangsar** is home to the city's affluent and trendy crowd. It is full of interesting cafés, eateries and shops, and at night, chic bars and watering-holes that are great for watching the beautiful people who come out to play. The biggest commercial area, **Bangsar Baru**, has trendy boutiques, cafés and restaurants clustered around the upmarket **Bangsar Village** (tel: 03-2282 1808; daily 10am–10pm). Sunday evenings see the area host a **night market** (*pasar malam*) with fresh produce and branded knock-offs. At the northern end of Jalan Maarof, 2km (1½ miles) away, is the **Bangsar Shopping Centre** (tel: 03-2094 7700; daily 10am–10pm). Other good, upmarket dining options are in the Jalan Bangkung and Lorong Kurau enclaves. For something quirky, check out the imaginative re-purposing of ex-printing works at **APW** (www.apw.my) on Jalan Riong for food, coffee and community events (see page 114).

Father and child at the National Mosque

Shop at the Islamic Arts Museum

Malaysia ⓫ (Islamic Arts Museum Malaysia; tel: 03-2274 2020; www. iamm.org.my; daily 10am–6pm). This spacious three-storey private museum is a dignified repository of artefacts from the Islamic world.

On the souvenir shop level look up to appreciate the beautiful white inverted dome with gold inscriptions of the opening verse of the Quran. It is one of the museum's five domes, which represent the five pillars of Islam.

Museum must-sees are the Malay World gallery, showcasing artefacts rarely found outside the region, and the intricate architectural models of famous monuments and structures of the Islamic era, including India's Taj Mahal and the famous mosques of the holy city of Medinah. Other displays include manuscripts, ceramics, textiles, jewellery and metalwork.

There are also facilities for kids as well as a great souvenir shop. Have a Middle-eastern meal at the **Museum Restaurant** (see ❸) or if you enjoy seafood, head back to the multi-storey carpark at the Botanic Garden's entrance to the **KL Seafood Market** (see ❹).

Food and Drink

❶ RESTORAN REBUNG CHEF ISMAIL

5-2, Level 5, Parkir Bertingkat Bukit Aman, 1 Jalan Tanglin; tel: 03-2276 3535; www.restoranrebungdatochefismail.com; daily 8am–10pm; $$
Owned by a celebrity chef, this restaurant offers a huge Malay buffet spread at lunch and dinner, complete with tasty desserts. Á la carte is available at breakfast and after 3pm.

❷ HORNBILL RESTAURANT & CAFÉ

Kuala Lumpur Bird Park, 920 Jalan Cenderawasih; tel: 03-2693 8086; www.klbirdpark.com; daily 9am–7pm; $
The fan-cooled veranda is a great spot to view the hornbills from. Try the fried *mee mamak*, spicy noodles with seafood and potatoes, or the best-selling chicken chop.

❸ MUSEUM RESTAURANT

Islamic Arts Museum Malaysia, Jalan Lembah Perdana; tel: 03-2092 7136; www.iamm.org. my; Tue–Sun 10am–5pm; $$$
Dine in sumptuous Moroccan surroundings on a set lunch menu, Mandy lamb or Moussaka. The delicious baklava and humus are also must-tries.

❹ KL SEAFOOD MARKET

5-1, Level 5, Parkir Bertingkat Bukit Aman, 1 Jalan Tanglin; tel: 03-2276 0066; www.facebook.com/klseafood; daily 11am–3pm, 6–10pm; $$
Cantonese-style seafood is served in this eatery, which has a nice outdoor seating area too. Crabs are the specialty here, but the salted egg squid and sang *har meen*, noodles with giant prawns are all well worth a try too.

Little India, Brickfields

BRICKFIELDS

Explore an old KL neighbourhood that, despite its Indian character, is also home to a lively multiracial community and diverse faiths. It is also in flux, and interesting for the questions it poses as to how steadfast it can be in the face of gentrification.

> **DISTANCE:** 2.5 km (2 miles)
> **TIME:** Half a day
> **START:** Sri Kandaswamy Kovil
> **END:** Jalan Tun Sambanthan
> **POINTS TO NOTE:** This is a walking tour best done in the morning or evening to coincide with Hindu prayer times. Take the Monorail to the Tun Sambanthan stop. Walk along Jalan Tebing for about 500 metres to the Sri Kandaswamy Kovil.

In the shadow of the ultra-modern transport hub of KL Sentral spreads **Brickfields**, a salt-of-the-earth neighbourhood that dates back to the 19th century, and represents a rapidly vanishing facet of KL. Being bestowed with a tacky 'Little India' label is not really saving it from 'urban regeneration', in the form of faceless towers mushrooming throughout the neighbourhood.

Development

In the late 19th century, the shantytown of early KL, with its wooden buildings, was very susceptible to fire. This led the colonial administration to decree that only brick structures were to be built from now on. As its name suggests, Brickfields was where the bricks to rebuild KL were manufactured, and the KL Sentral site was once a clay pit. Later on, the latter served as a railway marshalling yard.

Because of its proximity to KL town, Brickfields also became the site for housing railway and other government employees. Subsequently, a large number of schools and different religious buildings were erected.

SRI KANDASWAMY KOVIL

Brickfields was originally populated by mainly Tamils from southern India and Sri Lanka, who were brought to KL by the British to work in the Malayan Railways and the Public Works Department. Even today, Brickfields retains a very strong Indian character. Your first stop is at the end of Jalan Tebing, facing Jalan Scott. Here stands the **Sri Kandaswamy Kovil** ❶ (tel: 03-2274 2987; www.sri kandaswamykovil.org; daily 5am–1pm and 5–9pm; free), a temple founded by

Hindu temple carvings   *Deity in the Sri Kandaswamy Kovil*

the local Jaffna Sri Lankan community in 1909. The building, reconstructed in 1997, has a tall, elaborate *gopuram* (gateway). The key deity here is Lord Murugan, although the Mother Goddess Sri Raja Rajeswary, who is worshipped as the embodiment of love and grace and rarely found in similar Murugan temples, is also honoured here.

KRISHNA, HANUMAN AND MUNESWARAR

From the Sri Kandaswamy Kovil, continue on Jalan Scott, where Brickfields first took shape. In the early days, the road was filled with Chinese shops, Indian laundries, Chettier moneylenders, and spice and grocery shops that catered to the largely Indian population. On your right are three **Hindu temples** ❷ (daily 7am–noon, 7–11pm; free). The first is the humble Sri Krishna Temple, which honours the blue god and features a statue of him and two incarnations of his consort, Lakshmi.

Next door is the **Arulmegu Sree Veera Hanuman Temple**, which honours Hanuman, the Monkey God, revered for his courage and devotion. The temple houses five statues of the deity, which are worshipped with offerings of butter, applied to the mouth and tail, and garlands of *vadai*, a savoury fried fritter. The last of the temples is the Sri Maha Muneswarar Temple, where worshippers pray to Muneswarar, also known as Muni-andi, a guardian Tamil deity originally worshipped in plantations and villages.

WEI-LING GALLERY

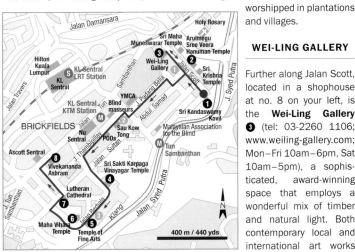

Further along Jalan Scott, located in a shophouse at no. 8 on your left, is the **Wei-Ling Gallery** ❸ (tel: 03-2260 1106; www.weiling-gallery.com; Mon–Fri 10am–6pm, Sat 10am–5pm), a sophisticated, award-winning space that employs a wonderful mix of timber and natural light. Both contemporary local and international art works

Indian food at Brickfields

are on display here. The shophouse was renovated by its previous owner, the renowned architect Jimmy Lim, for his artist daughter, Wei-Ling, who now runs the gallery. If you are feeling peck-ish, stop for a bite at the pleasant **Vishal Food and Catering** (see ①).

JALAN THAMBIPILLAY

Backtrack along Jalan Scott and turn right onto Lorong Padang Belia. At the end of the road, turn right again and then left onto Jalan Padang Belia. The road runs between a football field and some flats whose ground-floor shops are the last wholesaler holdouts. After about 500 metres, there is a junction that is hugged by the YMCA. Turn right and then left onto **Jalan Thambipillay**. Right at the corner outside Restoran One Sentral, look out for the **Brickfields Pisang Goreng Stall** (see ②) with its terrific banana fritters.

JALAN BERHALA

Continue on Jalan Thambipillay as it curves to the left, then turn left into Jalan Sultan Abdul Samad and right into **Jalan Berhala**. This U-shaped road was formerly known as Temple Road because of its large number of pre-World War II places of worship. Every Thursday, this street hosts a *pasar malam* (night market), which sells fresh produce and hawker fare. It has a great atmosphere and makes for a lovely evening stroll.

SRI SAKTI KARPAGA VINAYAGAR TEMPLE

A key temple on Jalan Berhala is the **Sri Sakti Karpaga Vinayagar Temple** ❹

Food and Drink

① VISHAL FOOD AND CATERING

22 Jalan Scott; tel: 03-2274 0502; daily 7.30am–10.45pm; $
This Chettiar family-run restaurant serves excellent traditional meals that contain subtle blends of sweet, sour and spicy. Try the rice with *sambar* (stew made from pulses) or the *puli kulambu* (tamarind curry). End with the sweet *payasam* (pudding).

② BRICKFIELDS PISANG GORENG STALL

Corner Jalan Tun Sambanthan 4 and Jalan Thambipillay; tel: 012-617 2511; noon–5pm; $
This stall is extremely popular for a good reason: the banana fritters are finger-licking good, and fried in front of you to boot. Other equally tasty savouries are also available.

③ ANNALAKSHMI RIVERSIDE CAFÉ

Temple of Fine Arts,112 Jalan Berhala; tel: 03-2274 3709; www.tfa.org.my; Tue–Sun 11.30am–9.45pm; $
Simple, home-style Indian vegetarian fare made by the volunteers at the centre, including breads and rice to go with dhal and curries; pay as you like.

(daily 6am–noon and 6–9.30pm, 6am–9.30pm during festivals; free). It is the country's only temple that hosts the Elephant God Vinayagar, also known as Ganesha, who holds a *sivalingam*, the symbol synonymous with the principal god Siva. This is a rare double-deity temple. In the Tamil month of Aavani, from August to September, Vinayagar Sathurthi, the festival honouring the Elephant God, is celebrated with morning prayers at the temple, followed by a parade of this statue in a chariot around Brickfields.

TEMPLE OF FINE ARTS

After another 200 metres is the **Temple of Fine Arts** ❺ (tel: 03-2274 3709; www.tfa.org.my; Tue–Sun 9.30am–12.30pm, 1.30–9pm; free), where you might hear the sound of ankle bells and tablas. This Indian cultural association has trained young Malaysians in traditional Indian dance and music, including some of the country's top performers. It stages signature large-scale and elaborate performances, as well as smaller shows. It also has a lovely gift shop and hosts the **Annalakshmi Riverside Café** (see ❸) and the fancier **Annalakshmi Restaurant**, both serving home-cooked vegetarian food.

MAHA VIHARA TEMPLE

Where Jalan Berhala curves again stands one of KL's most important Buddhist temples, the **Maha Vihara Temple** ❻

(tel: 03-2274 1141; www.buddhist-mahavihara.com; daily 6am–10.30pm; free). Temple devotees now include many non-Singhalese but all follow the Sri Lankan Theravada Buddhist faith. Modest in appearance and character on normal days, the temple assumes an electrifying atmosphere on Wesak Day in May (see page 25).

ZION CATHEDRAL OF THE TAMIL EVANGELICAL LUTHERAN CHURCH

From here, head back to Jalan Sultan Abdul Samad and turn right. At the corner is the **Zion Cathedral of the Tamil Evangelical Lutheran Church** ❼ (tel: 03-2274 1033; www.elcm.org.my; open Sun for services; free). This cathedral was established over a century ago, with roots in Indian, German and Swedish missions, the church holds services in Tamil, English and Indonesian.

VIVEKANANDA ASHRAM

Make your way to main road, Jalan Tun Sambanthan, to see the **Vivekananda Ashram** ❽, a long pink-and-white building, It was established for followers of the influential Indian spiritual leader of the Vedanta branch of Hindu philosophy, which is based on the most speculative and philosophical of Hindu scriptures. In front of this lovely colonial building is a statue of Vivekananda. Recently, this building has been threatened with re-development.

Jalan Masjid India

MASJID INDIA & KOTA RAYA

A historic Indian–Muslim quarter built on the textile trade that continues to be a vibrant shopping area. Meanwhile, down the road, a new migrant centre has taken root, another face of Malaysia's multi-faceted identity.

DISTANCE: 4km (2½ miles)
TIME: Half a day
START: Bank Negara Museum and Art Gallery
END: Telecommunications Museum
POINTS TO NOTE: Take the KTM Komuter to the Bank Negara stop or the LRT to the Bandaraya Station, then walk the 400 metres to the Bank Negara Museum and Art Gallery on Jalan Dato' Onn, which is where the tour begins.

Trade and commerce has shaped much of the Malay world for centuries and continues to do so today. This route explores these aspects of KL, first in a unique museum showcasing the history thereof, then to lively enclaves of Indian Muslim traders and former money-lenders, and finally, to an old migrant quarter, now the centre for new migrants.

BANK NEGARA MALAYSIA MUSEUM AND ART GALLERY

This museum of the **Central Bank ❶** (tel: 03-9179-2784; www.museumbnm.gov. my; daily 10am–6pm; free) is housed in a stunner of a building, which is architecturally influenced by the region's first currency, the shell, and overlaid with the diamond geometry of traditional textiles. Inside, learn about the global trade that helped build what is now Malaysia, as well as the country's development and continued role in global trade and finance markets. The exhibitions are interactive and well displayed. Climb the spiral 'nautilus' stairs, (which is an experience in itself), to reach the airy top floor of the museum, housing the bank's rotating art collection. The children's gallery is fun too. Commemorative coin collectors will love the souvenir shop.

Garment District

Masjid India, your next stop, is a 1km (½mile) walk away, so you may choose to grab a taxi instead. If not, head back to the KTM Komuter station. You will pass the memorial to the first Prime Minister of Malaysia, Tunku Abdul Rahman, housed in the century-old Residency where he once lived. At the station, cross over

Gold shop, Masjid India
Religious items for sale, Masjid India

to Jalan Raja Laut and then make your way between the towers to Jalan Tuanku Abdul Rahman. In the early 20th century, this road was dominated by tradesmen from the Indian sub-continent, and was the city's main shopping area, earning it the moniker of the 'Golden Mile'. Today, it is part of the garment district and is packed with wholesalers and retailers.

MASJID INDIA

Zig-zag your way through the lanes to Jalan Bunus 6, which intersects with

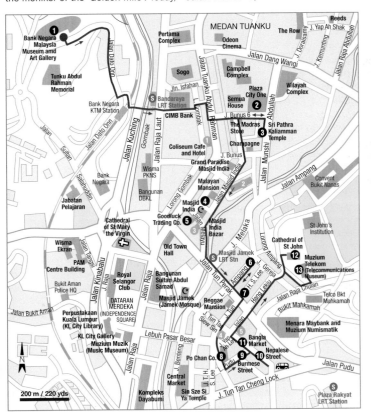

the top of **Jalan Masjid India**. Formerly sporting a marked Indian Muslim accent, Jalan Masjid India has become equally Malay over the years. Every space here is taken up by shops, eateries and colourful pavement stalls. There are Malay outfits, headscarves and sarongs, as well as Indian clothing and shoes, while elaborate gold jewellery from India and Dubai glitters in window displays.

Before heading down Jalan Masjid India, continue along Jalan Bunus 6. On the left is **Plaza City One ❷** (daily 9am–10pm), a one-stop shop for Malay weddings, with everything from fabrics and artificial flowers to costume rentals. Turn right into the lane parallel to Jalan Munshi Abdullah to visit a tiny but important temple in this area. Standing proud amidst the skyscrapers is the Hindu temple, **Sri Pathra Kaliamman Temple ❸** (daily 7–9.30am; 7–11.30pm). Its main deity is the green-faced Kali the Destroyer. Note the cobra-shaped worshipping paraphernalia in front and at the back of the temple; these are to appease a guardian spirit cobra. Many people from the surrounding areas, regardless of faith, pray at this temple.

From here, head back to Jalan Masjid India. The top of the road is flanked by two emporia named **Madras Stores** (daily 11am–8.30pm), each owned by former partners, and both meeting every need from pots and pans to spices and jewellery, and even Bollywood-style clothing and saris.

Walk down Jalan Masjid India and soak in the atmosphere. If you are feeling hungry, there are two choices. Turn right after the second block to head back to Jalan Tuanku Abdul Rahman and the colonial-era **Coliseum Café and Hotel** (see ❶). Otherwise, continue south and on your left behind the hawker centre is Selangor Mansion, where you will find an excellent vegetarian restaurant, **Saravanaa Bhavan**, (see ❷).

To your right is the brown-slate-covered **Masjid India ❹**, a 19th-century Indian Muslim mosque after which the street is named. It has been completely modernised but prayers are still conducted in Arabic and Tamil. The mosque is open only to Muslim worshippers, and on Fridays, everything comes to a standstill when the entire bazaar area and mosque surrounds are covered with prayer mats and filled with worshippers. There are good photo opportunities here, but do be discreet and respect the worshippers' right to privacy.

Continue along Jalan Masjid India and you'll reach a covered area, the **Masjid India Bazaar**. The bazaar sells mainly cheap stuff with a Malay and Islamic twist, including religious books and traditional herbal concoctions for health and beauty. Walk through the bazaar to reach Jalan Melayu and straight ahead is another food option, the iconic Punjabi eatery, the **Jai Hind Restaurant** (see ❸). To the right of this eatery at No. 7 is the **Goodluck Trading Company ❺** (tel: 03-2691 6006; Mon–Sat 9am–6.30pm), a whole-

Jalan Masjid India

saler set up by Chennai Indians in 1895. The shop is noted for its *kain pelikat chop gadja* hand-loomed sarongs from Pulicat in India. Afterwards, continue to Jalan Tun Perak.

LEBUH AMPANG

Turn left into Jalan Tun Perak and continue until you reach the next crossroads. This is **Lebuh Ampang** ❻, also known as Little India until the government decided the 'official' Little India was in Brickfields (see Route 5). Here, Indian money lenders once ruled the street and funded many local economic activities before World War II, which was the main recourse to credit for non-colonials. Though the money lenders are no longer around, a few of their early 20th-century shophouse offices have been left largely intact, complete with Greek columns, moulded plaster decorations and roof-level parapets. The area still has a distinctly Indian feel with a centre where the Indian sage Sai Baba is worshipped (No. 71), shops selling household goods and religious paraphernalia and restaurants galore.

Shophouse life
Head back to Jalan Tun Perak and turn left and then right into **Jalan Tun HS Lee** ❼ to experience more of the old KL shophouse life. There are still some old stores here but you can really feel the breath of change in the shape of establishments such as the flashpacker

Reggae Mansion on the corner. One business which has adapted to modern times and continues to do a roaring trade is the 70-year-old **Soong Kee Beef Noodle Shop** at No. 86 (see ❹), which started out as a hole-in-the-wall restaurant. Meanwhile, follow the left fork into Jalan Petaling to see the remaining goldsmith shops of this former 'Goldsmith Row'. Determinedly holding on are four remaining establishments, including **Po Chan & Co.** ❽ at No. 110 (tel: 03-2078 2763; Mon–Sat 10.30am–4pm), which has been selling locally-crafted products since 1912.

KOTA RAYA

As you continue to Kota Raya, you will begin start noticing signs with different characters. Named after a large shopping centre, Kota Raya has become an important home away from home for the estimated 200,000-strong migrant workforce on whom KL is so heavily reliant, including undocumented migrants and refugees. The migrants hail largely from Bangladesh, Myanmar and Nepal and the currency exchanged here is labour for cash. Kota Raya is prime example of history repeating itself: it is here where Chinese migrant labourers found a sense of community in a strange land during the 19th and 20th centuries.

Leases cannot legally be held by foreign workers, so each shop and eatery has a tiny counter selling mobile phones in the corner, the 'legitimate'

Cathedral of St John

business. Some shoplots are divided into numerous sublets, usually for a high price. The shops and pavements are bustling with people, mostly men, talking to each other, hanging out and buying betel nut from the hawkers who dot the pavements.

'Burmese' and 'Nepalese' Streets

From Jalan Petaling, turn left into Jalan Pudu, known as **Burmese Street ❾**. Here, you can browse through Burmese newspapers, shop for *lungyi* (sarongs), *thanaka* (sunscreen paste) and sample the Burmese national dish, *mohinga*, a fish noodle soup. Incidentally, the *lungyi* is a common denominator amongst all the migrants. Turn right into Jalan Tun Tan Siew Sin, and you will hit **Nepalese Street ❿**. Here, signboards in Devanagari script advertise haircuts, groceries, clothing and shoes. From the bus interchange on your left, you can take buses to middle-distance destinations such as Klang (Route 16).

Bangla Market

Turn back and go straight along Jalan Tun Tan Siew Sin. Continue to the **Bangla Market ⓫**. Here the smells of *gorom moshla* (Bengali spice mix) from numerous eateries permeate the air and you can hunt for the latest Bengali and Hindi-language blockbuster DVD as well as aromatic soaps and herbs. Look up at a tall building at No. 23 where a wholesaler has built a small mosque, Surau Al-Malik, for migrants. On the opposite corner of the block at No. 26 is the **Khukuri** (see ❺), a popular Nepali restaurant with great food.

CATHEDRAL OF ST JOHN

Turn right into Jalan Hang Lekiu and walk uphill for 500 metres towards the white church. The **Cathedral of St John ⓬** (tel: 03-2078 1876; www.stjohnkl.com.my; daily 6am–6.30pm; free) serves KL's Roman Catholic community. Sunday mass, which is held at 10.45pm, sees a large number of Filipino migrant workers, many of whom are maids; the Tahanang Filipino Ministry holds a mass in Tagalog every second Sunday. The church also caters to the pastoral care of migrant workers. Built in 1883, the

> ## Textile Currency
>
> Indian textiles were the currency of 15th- and 16th-century trade in the region. The textiles were brought to the Malay isles by Indian traders, who were mostly from Gujarat. The Indian producers also adapted their designs and styles to cater to local tastes and traditions. The two cloths that dominated the textile markets were chintz – both fine and coarse painted and dyed cottons – and *patola*, the Gujarati double-*ikat* silk cloth that also symbolised wealth. Today, India continues to be a major source of fabrics sold in Jalan Tuanku Abdul Rahman and Jalan Masjid India.

Muzium Telekom

building is in the shape of a crucifix and has lovely stained glass windows.

TELECOMMUNICATIONS MUSEUM

You tour ends at the **Muzium Telekom** ⓭ (Telecommunications Museum; tel: 03-2031 9966; daily 9am–5pm, closed public holidays), which can be found at the corner of Jalan Gereja and Jalan Raja Chulan. The museum is housed in one of KL's finest neoclassical buildings, c.1928, and provides a fascinating insight into the role and development of communications in local and global history, including an exhibit of artefacts that served locally as means of communications. The original telephone exchange the building was erected to house is also on display in its original location, as well as the actual switchboard. Textiles make a surprise appearance here too.

Food and Drink

① COLISEUM CAFÉ AND HOTEL

98–100 Jalan Tuanku Abdul Rahman; tel: 03-2692 6270; daily 10am–10pm; $$
Revisit the colonial days at this famous century-old bar and grill. Try a sizzling ribeye or baked crabmeat with salad. There are also firewood-baked English pot pies.

② SARAVANAA BHAVAN

1007 Selangor Mansion, Jalan Masjid India; tel: 03-2298 3293; daily 8am–11pm; $
Excellent Indian vegetarian food is served in a quiet, air-conditioned environment. The must-tries are the chilli *paneer* (spicy fried cottage cheese), cauliflower Manchuria and mushroom *roghan josh*.

③ JAI HIND RESTAURANT

11 & 13 Jalan Melayu; tel: 03-2692 0041; daily 9am–10pm; $
Customers laden with boxes of Punjabi sweets define this eatery, a 60-year-old Masjid India icon that also dishes up delicious home-style cooking such as the buffalo milk-*paneer* in spinach and the *dhaba* curry chicken.

④ SOONG KEE BEEF BALL MEE

86 Jalan Tun HS Lee; tel: 03-2078 1484; www.facebook.com/SoongKeeBeefNoodle; daily; Mon–Sat 11am–midnight; $
Old-school Hakka springy noodles are served here with juicy minced meat and a soup with tender beef balls. Its rice *congee* with chicken, pork or fish is also famously delicious.

⑤ KHUKURI

26 Jalan Tun Tan Siew Sin; daily 9am–9pm; $
Nepalese staples such as *momo* (filled steamed or fried dumplings) and *dal bhat* (lentil soup with rice) can be found on this first-floor outlet. Have it with the spiced *mahi* yoghurt drink and finish off with a fragrant *kheer* rice pudding.

Bukit Bintang

BUKIT BINTANG

In the city's main commercial district, shopping malls, chic boutiques, craft and heritage centres, acclaimed restaurants and nightlife venues vie for your attention. Find just about anything you desire in this bustling zone.

DISTANCE: 5km (3 miles)
TIME: Half a day
START: Kompleks Kraf
END: Jalan Alor
POINTS TO NOTE: This tour is recommended as an afternoon-to-evening itinerary, but start earlier if you enjoy shopping. To get to the Kompleks Kraf, take a taxi, the Hop-on Hop-off bus or the covered pedestrian walkway from the KLCC LRT station (20-minute walk).

True to its roots as the city's original entertainment quarter, Bukit Bintang today has the largest number of malls, restaurants and hotels per square metre in the city. Its retail offerings will satisfy even the most fanatic of shopaholics, while those less keen on shopping will have a craft centres, cafés, restaurants and watering holes to choose from.

CRAFT COMPLEX

Begin at the **Kompleks Kraf Kuala Lumpur ❶** (Kuala Lumpur Craft Complex; tel: 03-2162 7533; daily 9am–7pm; free) on Jalan Conlay. This one-stop craft centre is a government-run upmarket version of the Central Market (see page 37), with quality –and expensive – Malaysian textiles, ready-made wear and handicrafts. Besides a tiny **craft museum** (daily 9am–5.30pm), the complex houses a **Craft Village** where artisans work on batik artwork, ceramics and woodcraft – which are also for sale – and conduct classes for visitors. The complex occasionally holds handicraft fairs where there is a wider range of handicraft available; check the Tourism Malaysia website (www.malaysia.travel.com) for more details.

BADAN WARISAN

From Kompleks Kraf, walk along Jalan Conlay towards Jalan Raja Chulan. At the junction of Jalan Stonor sits a 1925 bungalow that houses the **Badan Warisan Malaysia ❷** (Heritage of Malaysia Trust; tel: 03-2144 9273; badanwarisanmalaysia.org; Mon–Sat 10am–5pm; free). This non-government organisation advocates the preservation and conservation

inside Pavillion Kuala Lumpur

Pavillion Kuala Lumpur

of the country's heritage. It holds talks, walks and events and houses a great resource centre (Tue–Sat 10am–4pm by appointment) as well as a gift shop with a range of cards and collectibles.

Headman's House

A highlight is the **Rumah Penghulu Abu Seman** (tours Mon–Sat 11am and 3pm), a beautiful traditional Malay timber house relocated from the northern state of Kedah. Formerly a headman's house, it was restored as an awareness-raising project.

BINTANG WALK

From Badan Warisan, continue on Jalan Conlay and turn left onto Jalan Raja Chulan at the junction. Cross the road to get to **Jalan Bukit Bintang**. Stretching 1km (1/2 mile) along the thoroughfare from the Pavilion shopping centre to the Lot 10 mall is a wide pedestrian mall known as **Bintang Walk ❸**. Lined with giant billboards, shopping centres, cafés and restaurants, it is a great area to buy stuff, dine and people-watch.

Pavilion Kuala Lumpur

The ritzy 550-outlet **Pavilion Kuala Lumpur** (tel: 03-2118 8338; www.pavilion-kl.com; daily 10am–10pm), hosts concept stores and entertainment outlets over eight precincts. Check out local couturiers with an international presence such

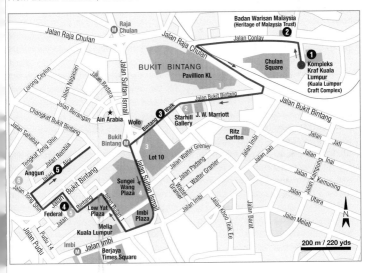

Batu Caves

BATU CAVES

The Batu Caves are home to a beautiful temple, one of the most important for Kuala Lumpur Hindus, and well worth the climb up the limestone massif. At its base are other shrines and a gigantic statue of Murugan.

DISTANCE: The Batu Caves are 13km (8 miles) from KL; the tour itself covers 4km (2½ miles)
TIME: 3 hours
START: Murugan Statue
END: Dark Caves
POINTS TO NOTE: Take the KTM Komuter to the Batu Caves stop. Do not fall prey to requests for entrance fees to the shrines. Admission is free; fees apply only to the art galleries. Women should make sure their legs are covered to enter the Temple Cave; otherwise, you will have to rent a pareo.

No visit to KL is complete without a trip to the **Batu Caves**. Established in 1891, the **Sri Subramaniar Swamy Temple** (tel: 03-6189 6284; www.batucaves.org) was originally just a cave temple in a wonderful setting, but has since expanded to include numerous temples.

MURUGAN STATUE

At the base of the Batu Caves is a 43 metre (140-ft) -**gilded statue of Murugan**, the largest of its kind in the world (with an equally large donation box). Hundreds of tonnes of concrete and steel bars and 300 litres (800 gallons) of gold paint were used to create the statue.

Food and Drink

1 RANI RESTAURANT
10 Batu Caves Temple; tel: 03-6186 2518; daily 7.30am–9.30pm; $
Serving vegan and *jain* food (no garlic or onion), Rani is known for its special *masala* tea (a milky tea infused with spices), excellent with the *masala thosai* (crepes filled with potatoes).

2 DHIVYA'S CAFÉ
9 Batu Caves Temple; tel: 03-6185 3788; daily 7am–9.30pm; $
Order the vegetarian burger, or the chicken or mutton alternatives to go with the banana leaf meal.

Thaipusam Festival   *Among the festival crowd*

TEMPLE CAVE

Behind the statue is the immense 272-step staircase that leads up to the **Temple Cave** (daily 8am–7.30pm, except Thaipusam, which is open 24 hours; free). Monkeys perch along the staircase up to the Temple Cave. They can be aggressive, so keep a safe distance and never feed them.

The large Temple Cave, measuring 80 by 100 metres (260 by 330ft), holds a shrine dedicated to Lord Murugan, who is known as a destroyer of evil and a dispenser of favours. Worshippers pray to a *vel*, Murugan's trident, which dates back to the temple's beginnings. Other deities are also honoured here.

SHRINES AND GALLERIES

Located in separate structures about 200 metres further to the left are shrines to Perumal and Anchaneyar, also known as Hanuman. The latter, the Monkey God, is a key character in the Indian epic, *Ramayana*, and is represented here by a 15 metre (50-ft) -tall statue.

You may also want to visit the **Cave Villa** (daily 8am–6pm), located to the left of the Murugan statue.

Rani Restaurant and **Dhivya's Café** both serve vegetarian Indian meals, see ❶ and ❷.

CAVE ECOLOGY

The Batu Caves Temple complex, which supports a fragile, unique ecosystem, is also of huge interest to cave ecologists and geologists. If you have sturdy shoes on, take the fascinating **Dark Caves Tour** (halfway up the steps to the Temple Cave; tel: 012-371 5001; www.darkcavemalaysia. com; Mon–Fri 10am–5pm, Sat–Sun 10.30am–5.30pm) and explore this unique ecosystem. The tour will take you 850 metres through a dark limestone chamber, and takes up to an hour.

[Map: Batu Caves area and Kuala Lumpur with scale 5 km / 3 miles, showing Selayang, Batu Caves Temple, Batu Caves KTM Station, Batu Caves, Gombak, Kepong, Sentul, Taman Sri Segambut, Batu, Wangsa Maju, Setapak, Setiawangsa, Kenny Hills, Keramat, Kuala Lumpur, Bukit Damansara, Bukit Bintang, Federal Hill, Chinatown, Taman Maluri, Ampang Jaya, Petaling Jaya, Rangsar, KL Sentral KTM Station, Pandan Indah]

Canopy walkway

FOREST RESEARCH INSTITUTE OF MALAYSIA

Discover a sprawling tropical rainforest located on the edge of the city. Part of a research institute, the forest holds star attractions such as a canopy walkway, a waterfall and splendid collections of old Malaysian trees.

DISTANCE: FRIM is 16km (10 miles) northwest of KL; the walk itself covers 4–6km (2.5–4 miles)
TIME: Half a day or a full day
START AND END: FRIM One-Stop Centre
POINTS TO NOTE: This is a half or full-day tour, depending on whether you enjoy being in the forest. The best time to visit is in the early morning or early evening when it is cooler, although the rainforest is usually shady any time of the day. Remember to drink lots of water and wear sturdy walking shoes. There are no direct bus services from KL to FRIM, so hire a taxi for the day (RM30 per hour). The closest KTM Komuter station is Kepong, where you can catch a taxi (RM15) to FRIM. Arrange with the taxi driver to pick you up at the end of the tour.

The oldest jungles in the world are the tropical rainforests of Southeast Asia and South America. Those who wish to visit a lush rainforest but do not want to travel too far out can head to the **Forest Research Institute of Malaysia** (FRIM; www.frim.gov.my; daily 5am–7.30pm), one of the world's oldest forest research centres, opened in 1929.

One-Stop Centre

Check in first at the **Information One-Stop Centre ❶** (tel: 03-6279 7592; daily 9am–4pm, except some public holidays). Staff can help you sort out your itinerary. There are several trails you can choose from, all of which require a guide (guides available Sat–Thu). You can also book guided tours by calling ahead. You can also rent bicycles from an operator outside FRIM (inside on weekends). If the Centre is closed, there are large maps throughout the area.

CANOPY WALKWAY

FRIM's most popular attraction is the **Canopy Walkway ❷** (Mon–Thu 9.30am–2.30pm), which winds high above the forest. This is a guided tour and visitor numbers are limited to 60 a day. Bookings must be made at least one day beforehand by email (frim_enquiry@

View from walkway

frim.gov.my). The tour will be cancelled if it rains.

Located up a steep climb to **Bukit Nolang** (489m/1,604ft), the Canopy Walkway is made of a secure network of ropes and ladders. It was built for scientists to study canopy-level flora and fauna. Anchored to five large trees, it stretches over 200 metres and suspends up to 30 metres (100ft) above the forest floor. There are platforms for rest and fantastic views along the walkway. At the canopy level, you can appreciate the multi-canopied structure of the rainforest. Each canopy is a sub-ecosystem on its own, with life forms that are different from those on the forest ground, such as shoots reaching high towards sunlight and insects pollinating flowers.

KERUING TRAIL

If you fancy a short nature walk, choose the 500-metre **Keruing Trail ❸**, which is next to the One-Stop Centre. This is the oldest of FRIM's trails and goes behind the museum among magnificent old timber trees. Be sure to pop into the **museum** (daily 9am–noon, 1–4pm; free), which has informative displays on forestry history and practices in Malaysia, together with research conducted by FRIM.

SUNGAI KROH

Otherwise, walk along Jalan Foxworthy for 1km (1/2 mile) to get to the **Sungai Kroh Picnic Area ❹**. A picnic in the forest is lovely, so buy water and snacks from the nearby **Rainforest & Nik Wan Café** (see ❶) or bring a picnic meal from the city. The beautiful streams and waterfall at Sungai Kroh are set among shady trees and great for

Map

500 m / 550 yds

Sungai Kroh Waterfall
Canopy Walkway ❷
★★

❹ Sungai Kroh Picnic Area
Rover Track

Salleh's Trail

Jalan Foxworthy

Forest Research Institute of Malaysia (FRIM)

Keruing Trail ❸

Dipterocarp Arboretum ❺
Engkabang Trail
Museum ❶

J. Symington
J. Jelutong
Coniferatum

Non-Dipterocarp Arboretum
J. Bkt Watson
Kroh
Sebasah Trail ❻
Ethno-Botanic Garden ❼

Jalan FRIM

J. Kapur
Wetlands
Fruit Tree Arboretum II

Entrance
Fruit Tree Arboretum I ★
❷

Sungai Kroh waterfall

splashing around in, particularly during the rainy season (Mar–May, Sept–Dec). You can also trek along the river uphill to another waterfall.

ARBORETUMS

When you are done, follow the Jalan Foxworthy loop round until you reach the start of the Engkabang Trail. This 550-metre trail takes you to the **Dipterocarp Arboretum** and the **Non-Dipterocarp Arboretum**.

These are among the seven arboretums in FRIM; large, open spaces planted with specific species, usually woody plants, for study and display. Of these, the **Dipterocarp Arboretum ❺** is world-renowned and contains some of the country's oldest and rarest trees, which are widely referenced by scientists. Dipterocarps are the largest tree family in Malaysia, covering almost three-quarters of its natural forested areas. If you have had enough, walk along Jalan Jelutong back to the One-Stop Centre.

Otherwise, if you feel like another couple of hours' walk, continue on to the 600-metre **Sebasah Trail ❻**, which takes you through wetlands and one of FRIM's two fruit tree arboretums where you will see mango, mangosteen and ficus trees. The trail ends at Jalan Kapur and joins Jalan FRIM, which will take you back to the One-Stop Centre.

ETHNOBOTANICAL GARDEN

If you have the time, visit the **Ethnobotanical Garden ❼** (you must book at the One-Stop Centre beforehand) on Jalan FRIM. These gardens showcase herbs that are traditionally used by indigenous people and various ethnic groups, together with species that have been introduced to the environment for economic and commercial reasons. Among them are the local viagra plants, *Tongkat Ali* and *Kacip Fatimah*, both of which have been locally commercialised.

If you've worked up an appetite during your tour of FRIM, you may want to enjoy a healthy meal at **BMS Organics Vegetarian Café** (see ❷) in Kepong.

Food and Drink

❶ RAINFOREST & NIK WAN CAFÉ

Jalan Foxworthy; Sun–Thu 9am–5pm; $
Selling mainly Malay fare, you can buy drinks and sandwiches or a packed nasi lemak for your hike, or have a hot meal here afterwards.

❷ BMS ORGANICS VEGETARIAN CAFÉ

G49E, Aeon Metro Prima, 1 Jalan Metro Prima, off Jalan Kepong; tel: 03-6250 8164; www.bmsorganics.com; Mon–Sat 11am–3.30pm, 5–8.30pm; $
A vegetarian eatery, serving natural and MSG-free food that is largely organic. Try its pumpkin fried rice or quinoa salads, served with a complimentary ginger drink. End with a dragon fruit-flavoured yoghurt.

Reservoir at the Sungai Selangor Dam

KUALA KUBU BHARU

*A playground for whitewater rafting, jungle-trekking, visiting
waterfalls and other nature-based activities, Kuala Kubu Bharu
and its peaceful surroundings are popular with day-trippers.*

DISTANCE: 72km (45 miles) north of
KL; the route itself covers 8km (5 miles)
TIME: A full day
START: Kuala Kubu Bharu
END: Chiling Waterfall
POINTS TO NOTE: Make this a day trip
or combine it with route 11 (Fraser's
Hill). By rail, take the KTM Komuter
from KL Sentral to Kuala Kubu Bharu.
From the station, there are private car
services (no taxis there) to take you to
town or to hire for the day. Alternatively,
rent a car from KL to self-drive,
particularly if you are headed also to
Fraser's Hill – it is a lovely drive.

Sungai Selangor flows for 110km (67
miles) through the state of Selangor
from the Titiwangsa Main Range into
the Straits of Malacca near the town of
Kuala Selangor. Like many other rivers,
it has charted the course of settlements,
including that of **Kuala Kubu Bharu ❶**.
KKB, as the locals call the town, is a
sleepy hollow en route to the highland
retreat of Fraser's Hill. Weekends see it

transformed into a busy stop-off point for
nature activities and adventure sports,
whether for meals or for stocking up supplies. The **Post Office Hawker Stalls**
(see ❶) are popular for breakfast; **Restaurant Ninety Eight** (see ❷) is good for
lunch and dinner; while **Teng Wun Bakery & Confectionary** is unmissable for
teatime snacks (see ❸).

WHITE WATER SPORTS

Different stretches of Sungai Selangor and
its tributaries are terrific for river activities
such as rafting and tubing, which involves
floating down the river in a rubber tube
– almost impossible to control, but a lot
of fun. Unless you have your own water
sports gear, it is best to join a tour organised by an adventure tour company (see
box). To get to the starting points of the
white water action, use the road leading
to Fraser's Hill. Part of this road skirts the
Sungai Selangor Dam, which supplies
water to parts of Selangor and KL. Along
the way, there are pleasant vistas of this
blue expanse of water and the surrounding 600-ha (1,480-acre) forested area.

Kayaking on the Chiling River

KAMPUNG GERACHI JAYA

Some of the most impressive views are from **Kampung Gerachi Jaya** ❷, atop a steep hill about 4km (2 miles) from KKB. This is the village of one of two indigenous Orang Asli communities that were relocated by the dam. The Orang Asli, who are from the Temuan group, now live in contemporary settlements which are a far cry from their former, forest-bound lives.

Always ask the Tok Batin, the village head, for permission to walk around in the village, and bring gifts of rice, biscuits or tea or coffee if possible. The Temuan speak little English and are very shy but are open to visits by tourists. These days, about half the Temuan earn an income through the collection and sale of jungle produce like bamboo and fruit to the townsfolk. Others work in rubber and oil palm estates and have odd jobs in town. White water sports and nature tourism have also given them a few skills and income opportunities.

KAMPUNG PERTAK

Drive on for another 3km (2 miles), and you will come to the other Temuan settlement, **Kampung Pertak** ❸. The houses are spread along the banks of Sungai Luit, a beautiful stream that tumbles over boulders large and small. Drive to the end of the village and walk down to the stream. The community charges a nominal fee to go upstream. If you don't fancy any strenuous activity, this is the perfect place to sunbathe, picnic and splash around in. Again, if you want to visit the village, do ask for permission first.

BUKIT KUTU AND WATERFALLS

If you are up for a trek, a trail leads beyond Kampung Pertak across a ramshackle bridge and up a right fork uphill to **Bukit Kutu** ❹. This is a challenging three-hour trek that winds through lovely forest and offers a 360-degree panorama of the surrounds from the top. Alternatively, take the left fork at the bridge to head to Lata Jebus Waterfall. If you keep going, another left fork

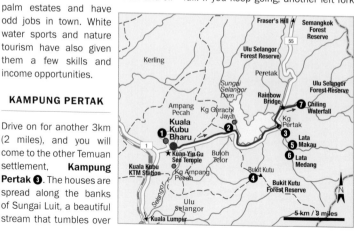

Playing on the Selangor River

Abseiling off the Rainbow Bridge

brings you to two other falls: The Lubuk and further on, the Lata Makau with its Olympic-sized pool. The trails are used by the Temiar people and are clearly marked (for more information, see www.waterfallsofmalaysia.com). However, jungle-trekking and waterfalls can be dangerous for the inexperienced, so hire a villager to guide you there or book with an adventure tour company. Avoid trekking after rainfall.

CHILING WATERFALL

A five-minute drive from Kampung Pertak is an old metal bridge known locally as the **Rainbow Bridge** because of its arched shape. Adventure sports operators sometimes use this bridge for abseiling activities. On the right side of the road is a trail marked by a gateway that leads to the lovely **Chiling Waterfall** ❺ (open Fri–Sun 8am–6pm). Getting there involves a 90-minute trek along the swift Sungai Chiling, a tributary of Sungai Selangor, and involves six river crossings. The sight of Chiling is well worth the trek: water falling 20 metres (66ft) into a very deep pool.

Adventure Sports

Adventure sports are risky, licensing for them poor and insurance is often non-existent, so check out the most current online reviews and ask questions about safety and training until you are satisfied. Recommended adventure sports operators include Pierose Swiftwater (white water rafting; tel: 013-361 3991; www.raftmalaysia.com), Primal Wilderness Experience (river tubing, abseiling, jungle-trekking; maximum 12 per group; tel: 016-206 7497; www.primalcreations.com) and OpenSky Unlimited (jungle-trekking; maximum 12 per group; tel: 012-350 1360; www.openskyunlimited.com).

Food and Drink

❶ POST OFFICE HAWKER STALLS

Jalan Abdul Hamid, opposite the post office; daily 6am–2pm; $

This row of 10 hawker stalls offers simple Malay and Chinese food. Try the wild-boar curry from stall no. 7 and steamed Chinese buns from stall no. 8.

❷ RESTAURANT NINETY EIGHT

33 & 34 Jalan Dato' Balai; tel: 03-6064 1198; Tue–Sun noon–11pm. $

Enjoy reliable Cantonese fare, such as wild-boar curry and the Hakka speciality of *khaw yoke*, thick slices of pork belly with yam, served in air-conditioned comfort.

❸ TENG WUN BAKERY & CONFECTIONARY

15, Jalan Dato Muda Jaafar; tel: 03-6064 1586; daily 8am–7pm; $

This famously friendly traditional Chinese bakery offers freshly-baked tasty butter sponge cakes, fragrant *kaya* puffs (coconut jam pastries) and fluffy cupcakes.

FRASER'S HILL

Enjoy highland weather and breathtaking views on this hill resort, which sits 1,500m (4,900ft) above sea level. Weekenders come here to unwind, explore jungle trails and tee off at the picturesque golf course.

DISTANCE: 104km (65 miles) north of KL; trails cover varying distances
TIME: A full day, or overnight
START/END: Information Centre
POINTS TO NOTE: It takes around two hours to get to Fraser's Hill from KL by road. An inter-state taxi costs about RM250 one-way. Alternatively, take the KTM Komuter to Kuala Kubu Bharu (see page 73) Rawang and a private car service from there to Fraser's (RM80). If you are planning on driving, check the latest road conditions with the information centre first.

British Malaya's first hill station, **Fraser's Hill**, attracts weekenders from KL with its cool weather (daytime temperature averages 20°C/68°F), misty, forested landscapes and serene atmosphere. It's great for escaping the lowland heat, but note that food, activities and accommodation options are limited and pricey; service is often as languid as the environment.

ROUTE 55

The road from KKB to Fraser's Hill is a scenic, thickly forested one that winds uphill. It is part of the historic first path built across the Titiwangsa Range, which is known as **Route 55** today. In the late 19th century, gold was transported by mule along this road from Raub, the then El Dorado of the peninsula, located on the east of the mountains, to Port Klang on the west coast via the old town of Kuala Kubu. One of the many who cashed in on the transport and supply provisioning on this road was the accountant-turned-mule-transport-entrepreneur Louis James Fraser. The hill was named after him, although he had long disappeared by the time the hill station was built in 1910.

Route 55 climbs up a slope. As you ascend, note the change in vegetation. Trees much shorter than the giants of the lowlands are common at these higher altitudes. At 1,200 metres (3,940ft), you will see more conifers and tree ferns.

The paddock

The Gap

At the base of Fraser's Hill, there are two turn-offs. The first is at **The Gap**, which is historically the gap between the boundaries of the states of Selangor and Pahang (Fraser's Hill is part of Pahang). It was also the mid-point on the mule-and-bullock-cart transport route during Louis Fraser's time. The Gap is used only by ascending vehicles; the other road is for descending vehicles.

COLONIAL BUNGALOWS

The resort is scattered over seven hills, on which sit English greystone bungalows surrounded by neat English gardens blooming with roses and hollyhocks. The tiny town centre around the clock tower, however, has some disastrous newer additions, while the modern high-rise hotels in the area have also failed to blend in with the landscape. The clock tower itself is actually a later mock-Tudor addition to the cluster of original colonial buildings, which are made up by the post office, police station and medical dispensary.

Check in at the Information Centre, which is at and run by **Puncak Inn ①** (tel: 09-362 2007; daily 8am–11pm), to get a free map and some advice on walking routes. Book ahead (Durai; mobile tel: 013-983 1633, office near Shahzan Inn; or Tourism Pahang; tel: 09-362 2195) for guided nature walks, birdwatching and night trekking.

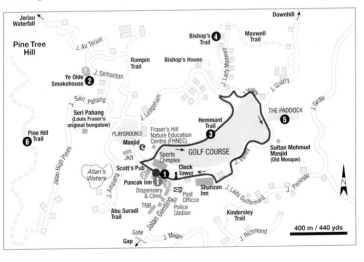

Giant fern at dawn

The Smokehouse

Follow Jalan Gap for 1.2km (3/4 mile) to the **Smokehouse Hotel and Restaurant ❷** (tel: 09-362 2226; www.the smokehouse.my), a Tudor-style concern built in 1924, complete with overstuffed chintz-covered sofas and a fireplace. It's falling apart a bit but those who really want an English tea-and-scone experience would enjoy this in its lovely garden (daily 3–6pm). The restaurant also serves the best, if slightly expensive, dinner in Fraser's Hill (see ❶).

WALKS

Because of its proximity to KL, Fraser's Hill is crowded at weekends, but there are enough walks and trails to take you away from the madding crowd.

Jeriau Waterfall

Turn left out of the Smokehouse Hotel and follow the road for about 4km (2 miles) to **Jeriau Waterfall**, a modest 10 metre (30-ft) -high waterfall that is both refreshing and a good location for bird-watching. Note that the steps leading to the waterfall are slippery after rain.

Golf Course

The ring road around the golf course makes for a pleasant two-hour walk, and brings you past the old bungalows and newer resorts. The picturesque nine-hole golf course is very old. It was carved out of an old tin mine, and is one of the few public courses in the country. You can rent golf sets and other accessories (tel: 09-362 2129; daily 8am–7pm).

JUNGLE TRAILS

There are also eight jungle trails of varying lengths, most well-marked and easy to follow.

Hemmant Trail

This is a longish route that takes in both the ring road and a short forest trail. From the Information Centre, take the same route as if you were heading to the Smokehouse. Follow it for about 200 metres until you see the sign for the **Fraser's Hill Nature Education Centre** on your right. Turn onto the road. This will bring you onto the **Hemmant Trail ❸**, which meanders for 2.5km (1.5 miles) through the forest before reaching the ring road again.

Bishop's Trail

When you reach the paved road, you have two choices: if you are in the mood for another forest trail, turn left and walk along the road until you come to the **Bishop's Trail ❹**, named after the clergyman who, in 1910, went looking for the missing Louis Fraser but failed to find him, and ended up establishing this hill retreat. This short trail has been turned into an interesting interpretive trail, complete with distance markers, informative signboards and learning stations.

Otherwise, to return to the town centre, turn right at the end of the Hemmant

The Bishop's Trail

Black-browed Barbet

Trail, where the paved road loops back to the starting point. The road skirts the golf course for most of the remaining 3km (1.5 miles). You'll pass a **paddock** ❺, where kids can ride a horse or try archery. Continue on this road until you reach the **town centre**.

Pine Hill Trail

If you are fit and experienced trekker, you may wish to take on the most challenging of the trails – the steep, guided-only 6-km (4-mile) **Pine Hill Trail** ❻, which peaks at 1,505 metres (4,938ft) above sea level and rewards those who conquer it with breathtaking views. The trail takes you through montane habitats abundant with vegetation and wildlife. As you ascend higher, you see the vegetation change.

BIRDWATCHING

The forests of Fraser's Hill have some of the richest birdlife in the peninsula. While on the trails, you may well bump into groups of avid birdwatchers standing completely still and peering intently through binoculars. There are an estimated 300 local and migratory species and this has put Fraser's Hill firmly on the birdwatching map. During the annual International Bird Race (tel: 09-568 7001; www.pahang-tourism.org.my), which is usually during the middle of the year, international birdwatchers descend on the area and race to identify the largest number of bird species on the official checklist.

Dining Options

There are a couple of grocery shops (daily 9am–10pm) in the town centre. For meals, try **Hill View Restaurant** (see ❷), for Chinese food, or **Scott's Pub** (see ❸) for Malaysian and European food.

Food and Drink

❶ SMOKEHOUSE HOTEL AND RESTAURANT

Jalan Jeriau; tel: 09-362 2226; www.the smokehouse.my; daily dinner 6.30–9.30pm; $$$$

This does a good job with traditional English fare such as pot roasts and Yorkshire puddings. Classical music and a log fire add to the quaint atmosphere. No shorts and sandals.

❷ HILL VIEW RESTAURANT

Puncak Inn; tel: 09-362 2231; daily 10.30am–8.30pm; $

Operated by a local family who have been residents on the hill for two generations, this serves Chinese meals and decent pub grub. The chicken and lamb chops are highly recommended.

❸ SCOTT'S PUB

Jalan Genting, near Puncak Inn; tel: 09-362 2226; daily noon–10pm; $

Located in a colonial building by the clock tower, it has a modest menu that includes a decent chicken or lamb chop and fish and chips, as well as beer.

The Skyway

GENTING HIGHLANDS

Perched on the Titiwangsa Range 1,870 metres (6,120ft) above sea level, Genting Highlands is Malaysia's Las Vegas. The kitschy resort draws families, gamblers and day-trippers looking for respite from the lowland heat.

DISTANCE: Genting Highlands is 51km (32 miles) northeast of KL
TIME: A full day, or overnight
START: Skyway station
END: Chin Swee Caves Temple
POINTS TO NOTE: The Genting Highlands Resort (www.rwgenting.com) offers all manner of packages from day-tours to overnight packages, including transport, accommodation and entry to attractions. By bus, it is 1 hour from KL Sentral; the fare is inclusive of the cable-car transfer. The daytime temperature hovers around 15–25°C (59–77°F).

Genting Highlands is the successful rags-to-riches story of migrant Lim Goh Tong, who built what is today a popular entertainment complex which draws 20 million tourists a year and a US$6 billion global conglomerate.

SKYWAY

The start of your Genting experience is the cable-car ride which glides above a blanket of montane vegetation. There are two options: the **Genting Skyway** ❶ (3.4km/2.1 miles in 11 minutes) from the Gohtong Jaya station and the **Awana Skyway** ❷ (2.8km/ 1.7 miles in 10 minutes) from the Awana Transport Hub; the latter has 10 glass-bottomed gondola

Food and Drink

❶ COFFEE TERRACE

Lobby Level, Genting Grand; tel: 03-6101 1118; breakfast 7–10.30am, lunch noon–2.30pm, dinner 5–9.30pm; $$
A wide variety of buffet options are available here, from local and fusion fare to Thai, Japanese and continental. It is huge, seating 600, but is well spread out and spacious.

❷ SPICE GARDEN

Lobby Level, Genting Grand; tel: 03-6101 1118; daily noon–midnight; $$$
This restaurant has stood the test of time and continues serving well-prepared North Indian and Middle Eastern dishes. Try the tandoori prawns and mutton *roghan josh*.

First World Plaza

Chin Swee Temple

options for the stout of heart, and stops at the Chin Swee Temple (see 6 below).

CASINO

Within the Genting Grand Hotel is the **Casino de Genting** ❸ (daily 24 hours; minimum age 21), on the first floor, for table games, slots and keno. The dress code is long trousers and collared shirt or t-shirt, or the traditional Malaysian batik shirt for men. Sandals and caps are not allowed; neither are mobile phones nor cameras. Muslims are forbidden to enter.

FIRST WORLD INDOOR THEME PARK

Over at the **First World Plaza** is the **First World Plaza Indoor Theme Park** ❹ (Mon–Fri 10am–midnight, Sat 9am–1am, Sun 9am–midnight), with video games, family and children's rides, a Snow World and Ripley's Believe It Or Not. There are also two cinema halls and a 28-lane bowling alley (Mon–Fri noon–midnight, Sat–Sun 10am–midnight) which has lanes for glow-in-the-dark bowling (daily from 6pm).

SHOPPING AND ENTERTAINMENT

Shoppers will enjoy browsing through the **Sky Avenue Mall** ❺. There are 90-odd eateries in the resort to choose from, including food courts, fast-food outlets and fancy restaurants. Try the **Coffee Terrace** or the **Spice Garden** (see ❶ and ❷). If you are staying overnight, watch a show in the evening: there are three theatres in town, featuring cabaret dinner shows, musicals and concerts.

CHIN SWEE TEMPLE

For some peace and quiet, take the free shuttle from the resort to the **Chin Swee Caves Temple** ❻ (daily 24 hours; free). Perched on a steep slope, the temple honours the Reverend Chin Swee, who purportedly inspired Gentings' founder, to build the resort. Carvings on the outside walls depict Chin Swee's life and his statue sits in the main chamber.

An elephant and its trainer

KUALA GANDAH

Visit a forest recreational park before seeing Asian elephants up close at the Kuala Gandah National Elephant Conservation Centre. Nearby is Kampung Kuala Ganlah, home to the Che' Wong indigenous community.

DISTANCE: Kuala Gandah is 120km (75 miles) northeast of KL
TIME: A full day
START: Hutan Lipur Lentang
END: Kuala Gandah National Elephant Conservation Centre
POINTS TO NOTE: Hire a car or taxi (RM250 for a round trip). Take the Karak Highway towards Kuantan. Budget two hours for the other attractions so you can reach Kuala Gandah by 11am. Bring a change of clothes if you intend to get into the river with the elephants.

The **Karak Highway** is a beautiful road that snakes up the Titiwangsa Range, making for a nice drive. As you climb, breathtaking scenery unfolds – dramatic mountains clothed in lush tree cover are framed by azure skies.

HUTAN LIPUR LENTANG

From the Gombak toll, drive for about 30km (18.5 miles) until you see an exit on your left at KM48, signposted **Hutan Lipur**

Lentang ❶ (Lentang Forest Recreational Park; free). Turn off here, drive under the highway, turning left again to get to the park. On the right is the office of the **Forestry Department** (tel: 09-2330 484; Mon–Fri 8am–5pm, Sat–Sun 10am–5pm), which manages the park. Pack food from the city or from the food stalls (8am–5pm) and picnic under the shady trees along the cold, swift stream.

KAMPUNG KUALA GANLAH

Get back onto the Karak Highway and drive for another 50km (31 miles) before exiting at Lanchang. After 13km (8 miles),

Food and Drink

❶ RESTAURANT FOON LOKE

84 Kampung Bukit Tinggi; tel: 09-233 0170; daily 10.30am–10pm; $
This no-frills eatery is famous for its vermicelli with prawns, which is served in a rich ginger broth. It also makes a mean stuffed tofu and stir-fried home-grown vegetables.

Feeding time

you reach a village on your left. This is **Kampung Kuala Ganlah ❷**, home to the Che' Wong, an Orang Asli indigenous group who reside in Central Pahang. A large triangular hut houses a handicraft centre (daily 10am–1pm), where you can buy baskets and bangles woven by the women of the 150-member community.

NATIONAL ELEPHANT CONSERVATION CENTRE

Down the road is the **Kuala Gandah National Elephant Conservation Centre ❸** (tel: 013-908 8207; www.wildlife. gov.my; daily 10am–4.45pm). The centre serves as a temporary base for elephants that are being relocated from one place to another. Translocation is a key

mechanism to prevent human-elephant conflict when forests are cleared for agriculture and elephants get killed by angry planters. Older elephants are relocated to state and national parks, but unfortunately babies almost never adapt again to the wild and are sent to zoos.

Note that the animals you will see are captive. They can never live in the wild again due to injury or inability to be rehabilitated. They have been trained to interact with people; wild animals awaiting translocation are not on display. After you register, head to the activity centre where you can hire a local guide to tell you about elephant conservation.

En route back to KL, stop at **Restaurant Foon Loke** (see ❶) in Bukit Tinggi for hearty Chinese food.

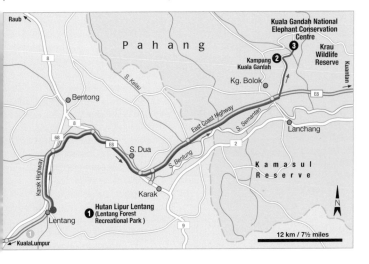

Bukit Melawati

KUALA SELANGOR

Defined by its coastal location, Kuala Selangor charms with its historical sights and unique mangrove ecosystem, birdwatching opportunities, fresh seafood and a riverside that is ablaze with fireflies at night.

DISTANCE: Kuala Selangor is 67km (42 miles) northwest of KL; the tour itself covers 16km (91 miles)
TIME: A full day, or overnight
START: Bukit Melawati
END : Kampung Kuantan
POINTS TO NOTE: Hire a car or taxi to get to Kuala Selangor 1 hour's drive from KL. Head north on the North-South Expressway, exit at Sungai Buloh and follow the road for 45 minutes until you reach the Assam Jawa junction, where you turn right. Drive for about 10 minutes until you reach Bukit Melawati and the old Kuala Selangor town centre. Unless you want to spend more time at the Nature Park, get to Bukit Melawati by the early afternoon so you end the excursion with the night-time firefly tour. Tours from KL include transport, the sights in this itinerary and seafood dinner and cost around RM300.

Located at the estuary of the Selangor River, Kuala Selangor was once the capital of the Sultanate of Selangor. The river was a vital means of communication to the otherwise impenetrable interior. It was also the key to political and economic power: those who controlled communications along the river also controlled the hinterland. The state of Selangor had three great river systems – the Langat, Klang and Selangor – and the respective nobilities who controlled these rivers fought constantly for dominance. Ultimately, the group that controlled the Klang became the strongest.

BUKIT MELAWATI

Whatever greatness the town of Kuala Selangor once enjoyed is still apparent on **Bukit Melawati** ❶. The historic hill is located in the old town and directions to it are well signposted. The 1.5km (.75-mile) road around the hill, with huge century-old raintrees and nice lookouts of the surroundings, makes for a pleasant walk. Keep left every time you come to a fork.

Historical Remnants
The second Sultan of Selangor built a fort on Bukit Melawati to repel attacks from

the Dutch during his reign (1778–1826). The Dutch captured the fort briefly but thereafter many bloody battles were fought over it. As you walk up the hill, you first pass a **poison well**, once filled with a poisonous mixture of latex and juice from bamboo shoots for torturing traitors. Further along on your right is the Dutch-built **Altingsburg Lighthouse**, opposite which is a **lookout** with great views over the Kuala Selangor Nature Park. Peering over the lookout are six **canons** from the Selangor-Dutch war. The **watchtower** here is where Muslim religious authorities traditionally sight the new moon during key dates in the Muslim calendar, such as the beginning and end of Ram-

adan. Walk on and you will come to the remains of the **Melawati Gate**, the former gateway to the fort.

The last attraction is the **Royal Burial Ground** of the first three Sultans of Selangor and their families. Entry to the mausoleum is restricted, but if you peer through the gates, you will see the **Penggawa**, the sacred canon draped with yellow cloth and the sultans' most trusted protector.

Return to the Melawati Gate and descend the steps down to the foot of the hill. Dubbed **The Hundred Steps**, these were once the only pathway to Kuala Selangor town from the dock below. The dock area is now the Kuala Selangor Nature Park. Turn right and

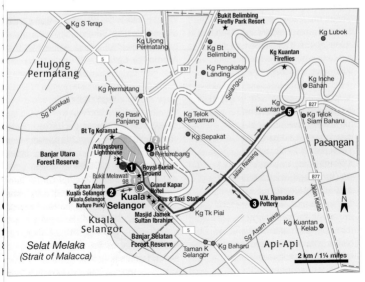

Wat Chetawan

PETALING JAYA

Located southwest of KL, Petaling Jaya is typified by sprawling housing estates and small town centres, but it also boasts an excellent museum and conservatory, and a thrilling water theme park.

DISTANCE: Petaling Jaya is 20km (13 miles) southwest of the city centre; the tour itself covers 15km (9 miles)
TIME: A full day
START: Wat Chetawan
END: Sunway City
POINTS TO NOTE: Take the LRT to Taman Jaya and hire a taxi for half a day. You can walk the 1km (1,760ft) to the first stop, but will still need to hire a taxi from there. If you forgo Sunway City, complete the first half of the tour in the morning and continue with Route 16 (Klang), 17 (Pulau Carey) or 18 (Putrajaya). Do this tour on a weekday, as the Universiti Malaya attractions are closed on weekends.

Petaling Jaya offers a look at suburban Malaysia. Originally developed as a low-cost housing scheme in the late 1950s, today PJ is a middle-class city that is home to over half a million people.

WAT CHETAWAN

Glinting roofs welcome you to the Sia-mese temple complex, **Wat Chetawan** ❶ (Jalan Pantai 9/7; tel: 03-7955 2443; www.sites.google.com/site/watchetawan; daily 6.30am–8.30pm; free). One of the few royal-sponsored temples outside Thailand, this is a religious community centre for Malaysian Thais, although its devotees also include non-Thais.

The *wat* (or temple) is impressive for its steep multi-tiered orange-tiled roofs, whose ends are decorated with curling ends called *chofah*. The buildings also feature intricate carvings, miniature glass tiles and the liberal use of gold. The main prayer hall houses several Buddha images. Open-sided pavilions dot the grounds, including of a four-faced statue of Buddha and Guan Yin, the Goddess of Mercy. A smaller hall pays tribute to Buddhist abbots, featuring Malay titles, reflecting their northern peninsular Malaysian and southern Thai origins.

From here, walk or drive 800 metres north on Jalan Gasing for Hainanese food at **1977 Ipoh Chicken Rice** (see ❶) or an Indian brunch at **Kana's Restaurant** (see ❷).

Museum of Asian Art *Orchid conservatory*

MUSEUM OF ASIAN ART

Move on to Universiti Malaya, the country's premier university, to visit three attractions. The **Museum of Asian Art ❷** (Muzium Seni Asia; tel: 03-7967 3805; www.museum.um.edu.my; Mon–Thu 9am–1pm, 2–5pm, Fri 9am–12.15pm, 2.45–5pm; free; book ahead for a guided tour) is a gem showcasing 6,000 pieces of art – mainly ceramics – spanning 4,000 years of Malaysian and Asian history. The museum's *kendi* (a water container with a spout and no handles) collection is the world's largest public collection of its kind, covering 1,000 years. The containers' shapes and designs are clues to cultural and social practices and trade patterns of East and Southeast Asia.

Chancellery

Take Lingkungan Budi to your next stop, passing the home of the university's former chancellery, the **Dewan Tunku Canselor**, on your right. This building is influenced by the style of the 1950s architect Le Corbusier, and is typical of the era when functionality, instead of indigenous design, reigned supreme over Malaysia's institutional buildings.

A right turning past this building brings you to the new chancellery building, which is home to the Universiti **Malaya Art Gallery ❸** (UMAG; tel: 03-7967 3805; Mon–Thu 8am–5pm, Fri 8am–12.15pm, 2.45–5pm; free). This houses the university's collection of largely local paintings and sculptures from the 1960s–1980s. However, it also appeals

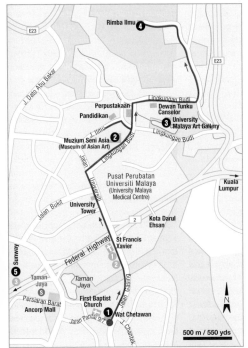

to non-traditional gallery visitors through funky, contemporary and experimental rotating exhibitions.

RIMBA ILMU

About 500 metres from the chancellery turn left at a fork. Continue for another 1.5km (1 mile) and you will reach the **Rimba Ilmu Botanic Garden** ❹ (tel: 03-7967 4685; rimba.um.edu.my; Mon–Thu 9am–4pm, Fri 9am–noon and 2.45–4pm), also known as the Forest of Knowledge. This botanical garden is one of the most important biological conservatories in Malaysia. Begin at its excellent interpretive exhibition on rainforests and the environment, then stroll through **The Garden**, a 45-minute walk through five collections: medicinal plants, palms, citrus and citroids (lime family), ferns and bamboo.

SUNWAY

From Rimba Ilmu, get onto the Federal Highway and drive towards Klang. After about 10km (6 miles), turn off onto **Sunway** ❺.

Sunway Lagoon

This development, built on rehabilitated tin-mining land, hosts the popular **Sunway Lagoon Water Theme Park** (tel: 03-5639 0000; sunwaylagoon.com; daily 10am–6pm). Inspired by South Africa's Sun City, this family-friendly venue is spread over 32ha (80 acres) and has six different theme parks and a huge man-made surf beach, complete with artificial waves.

Sunway Pyramid

The adjoining **Sunway Pyramid** (tel: 03-7492 9998; www.sunwaypyramid.com; daily 10am–10pm) is a huge Egyptian-themed shopping mall anchored by a giant lion in a sphinx-like pose. Besides hundreds of shops and eateries, the mall has an indoor ice-skating rink, a 12-screen cineplex and 48-lane bowling alley. Outdoor cafés line the front of the mall, serving everything from American coffee to sushi and hawker fare.

Food and Drink

❶ 1977 IPOH CHICKEN RICE

107 Jalan Gasing; tel: 03-7956 0958; www.facebook.com/1977ipohchickenrice; daily 9am–10pm; $

This long-standing restaurant serves great Hainanese chicken rice: fluffy rice flavoured with chicken stock and accompanied with steamed or roasted chicken; crunchy bean sprouts are a nice side order.

❷ KANNA CURRY HOUSE

109 Jalan Gasing; tel: 03-7958 4345; www.kannacurryhouse.com; daily 7am–10pm; $

Tuck into rice and delicious breads with various different South Indian curries, pickles and crispy *papadom* wafers. Its *vadai* lentil cakes and curry puffs are not to be missed. Wash it down with a hot or iced ginger tea.

Masjid Bandar Diraja Klang

KLANG

Klang Valley's liveliest Indian quarter is in Klang, a royal town with gems of quirky architecture from the British colonial era, interesting nooks, and home to a unique pork dish.

DISTANCE: Klang is 32km (20 miles) from KL; the morning tour covers 4km (1.5 miles)
TIME: A full day
START: Masjid Sultan Sulaiman
END: Jalan Tengku Kelana
POINTS TO NOTE: Take the KTM Komuter to Klang (1 hour). The morning route is a walking tour, after which you may choose to visit Pulau Ketam or continue with Route 17 (Pulau Carey) or 18 (Putrajaya). Alternatively, combine it with Route 14 (Kuala Selangor) or 15 (Petaling Jaya). To get to the other routes, hire a non-metered taxi from the KTM station; the rate should cover the return trip and the waiting fee of RM30 per hour.

Southwestwards from Petaling Jaya, the rest of the Klang Valley conurbation roughly follows the Klang River as it flows towards and decants into the sea at Port Klang, Peninsular Malaysia's main port. The word 'Klang' is thought to be of Mon-Khmer origin, meaning 'waterway'.

Klang

About 10km (6 miles) inland from the port is Klang, an old settlement that dates back to prehistoric times, though there is no trace of that today. Named after the river, **Klang**, the one-time capital of Selangor, was, in fact, one of several capitals of the state of Selangor, two others being Kuala Langat and Kuala Selangor. In earlier times, the warlords of each capital attempted to establish their hegemony, but the 1867 Selangor Civil War established Klang's dominance and consequently led to its development as a major city, fuelled in the early days by tin, a precious commodity at the time. Today, Klang continues to wear the badge of royal city and development-wise, is catching up with its more built-up neighbours, Shah Alam, the current capital of Selangor, and Petaling Jaya.

MASJID SULTAN SULAIMAN

Your first stop, the golden-domed **Masjid Sultan Sulaiman** ❶ (Sultan Sulaiman Mosque; daily 8–11am; free) is about 1km (.5 mile) from the Klang KTM

Sultan Abdul Aziz Royal Gallery

Komuter station. To get there, walk or take a taxi down Jalan Kota Raja. Built by the British in 1932 as a gift to Sultan Alauddin Sulaiman Shah, who was also a knight of the British Empire, it has an eclectic blend of neoclassical, Mughal and Arabic architectural styles, complete with colourful stained-glass features. To the left of the mosque is a peaceful royal mausoleum. To enter the buildings, check with the guard first and make sure your arms and legs are covered; women must also have their hair covered.

COLONIAL BUILDINGS

Head back towards the KTM station. At the junction of Jalan Dato Hamzah and Jalan Stesen are two historic buildings. On the left is the former **Standard Chartered Bank building ❷**, completed in 1874 in a neo-classical style. During World War II, it was used by the Japanese army as an interrogation centre. It's now a sari emporium. On the right is the former colonial administration office. Turn right into Jalan Stesen to get to the entrance of the building, now the **Sultan Abdul Aziz Royal Gallery ❸** (tel: 03-3373 6500; www.galeridiraja.com;

Tue–Sun 10am–5pm; free). Designed by the same architect as the Masjid Jamek in KL's Heritage Quarter, the gallery showcases various historical memorabilia of the Selangor sultanate.

BAK KUT TEH

Next, walk towards the train station and turn left into Jalan Besar. There are some well-preserved pre-war shophouses here. Just before the flyover, try some Klang *bak kut teh*, the herbal pork soup synonymous with the town. Believed to

Klang market   *Little India on Jalan Tengku Kelana*

have been brought to the Malay Peninsula from Fujian, China, by an immigrant, it is now widely available across the country. **Restoran Seng Huat** (see ①), known as 'the restaurant below the bridge', serves it for breakfast and dinner. The dining experience is quite interesting, so give it a try.

GEDUNG RAJA ABDULLAH

After your hearty meal, walk under the flyover and turn left into Jalan Gedung Raja Abdullah. On your right is the **Gedung Raja Abdullah** ❹, a warehouse-cum-home built in 1856 by Raja Abdullah, one of the two local chieftains who were involved in the Selangor Civil War. This is the last of Klang's historical tin-related buildings, the lucrative metal that was behind much bloodshed and British interference in local affairs. Typifying the traditional Malay architecture of that period, the building served in modern times as a tin museum but has been closed for renovations for many years now. From the Gedung Raja Abdullah, walk towards the large blue mosque and past the pretty Victorian-era fire station, to get to **Jalan Tengku Kelana**.

RELIGIOUS ENCLAVE

The mosque is **Masjid India Klang** (Klang Indian Mosque), first built in 1910 for the Indian Muslim merchant community. However, all that's left of the old structure is a tiny gateway which you will see when you turn right into Jalan Dato Hamzah. The current mosque has elements of South Indian mosque architecture. Continue along this road and take the left fork to explore this area of **100-year-old religious institutions** ❺. These churches and temples were established to cater to migrant workers in Klang and its surrounds. Today, they serve healthy local congregations and in the case of the churches, continue evangelising to migrants today, whereby mass and bible classes are conducted in numerous languages, including Vietnamese, Burmese and Telegu.

Methodist churches

Walking along this road, you will come first to a Mandarin-language Methodist kindergarten adjoining the steeple-roofed **Tamil Methodist Church** (www.tmcklang1908.wordpress.com). Next to that is an Anglican church named after missionary **St Barnabas** (www.sbck lang.org). Turning left and heading up Jalan Bukit Jawa for 120 metres (400ft) takes you to the **Wesley Methodist Church** (www.klangwesley.com).

Meanwhile, further up the hill is the **Gurdwara Sahib Klang** (www.facebook. com/Gurdwara-Sahib-Klang-16199 1327164998), the main place of worship for Klang's Sikhs, who, like other Malaysian Sikhs, are descendants of British Malaya policemen.

Sri Nagara Thendayuthapani Temple

Head back down to Jalan Tengku Kelana.

Street vendor selling Indian sweets, Klang

At the junction, you will see a Hindu temple straight ahead with an impressive *goparam* (gateway). This is Klang's oldest Hindu temple, the 150-year-old **Sri Nagara Thendayuthapani Temple** ❻ (tel: 03-3372 0748; daily: 7–11.30am, 6–9pm; free). This Chettiar-run temple has as its main deity the goddess Durga, whose key festival is the Vijayadasami in November, when gratitude is expressed for success. Other deities in the temple are Amman, Krishna and Murugan.

Food and Drink

❶ RESTORAN SENG HUAT BAK KUT TEH
9 Jalan Besar; tel: 012-309 8303;
www.senghuatbakkutteh.com; daily
7.30–12.30pm, 5.30–8.30pm; $
Located in an old *kopitiam*, this popular Klang *bak kut teh* eatery dishes up a hearty meaty and herbal soup. Various cuts of pork are available; the soup is usually accompanied by rice and Chinese tea.

❷ SRI BARATHA MATHA VILAS RESTAURANT
34 Jalan Tengku Kelana; tel: 03-3372 9657; daily 6.30am–10.30pm $
Prepared using an original house recipe for over 50 years; the signature spicy Indian *mee goreng* fried noodles are served with slices of crispy battered prawn cakes, tofu and egg. Great with a cold, freshly squeezed lime juice.

LITTLE INDIA

From here, backtrack to **Jalan Tengku Kelana** ❼. This road and its vicinity make up the most vibrant Little India in the Klang Valley. From spices to saris and music to *muruku* (deep-fried snacks), the colours, cacophony and aromas of this ethnic enclave assault the senses from all corners.

A good spot for an authentic Indian meal is **Sri Baratha Matha Vilas Restaurant** (see ❷), whose speciality is *mee goreng*, a spicy and delightfully sweet fried noodle dish.

Klang Valley residents know Jalan Tengku Kelana is the best place to shop for Indian goods and services, including arranging flights to India, sari-tailoring and fortune-telling. If you enjoy shopping or taking photographs, you can easily spend a couple of hours here. The atmosphere here during Diwali, the Hindu Festival of Lights, is electrifying.

PULAU KETAM

Off the coast of Selangor is a popular local destination, **Pulau Ketam** (Crab Island). To get there, take the KTM Komuter to Pelabuhan Klang (Port Klang), followed by a 30-minute ferry to the island. Everything on the island revolves around fishing, whether it is catching or rearing fish, or transport and support services. End your visit with Chinese-style meal of fresh seafood at any of the restaurants on the island.

A shaman prays on the beach

PULAU CAREY

In the Mah Meri community on Pulau Carey, the men carve beautiful woodcarvings born of dreams while the womenfolk make traditional woven products. Further on is Jugra, an old capital of Selangor, with a few historical relics that remind us of its royal past.

DISTANCE: 60km (37 miles) southwest of KL. Pulau Carey to Jugra is about 20km (12½ miles)
TIME: Half a day
START: Pulau Carey
END: Jugra
POINTS TO NOTE: From KL, take the KTM Komuter to Klang. Hire a taxi from the station and get onto Route 5 towards Banting. After about 24km (9 miles), you reach Teluk Panglima Garang and a roundabout. Follow the signs to Pulau Carey. After 1km (½ mile), look out for a sharp right turn: this road takes you across a bridge to Pulau Carey. You can combine this route with Route 16.

This is an opportunity to visit what is the Klang Valley's last original indigenous woodcarvers' village, located in an oil palm plantation on Pulau Carey (Carey Island).

KAMPUNG SUNGAI BUMBON

About 9km (5.5 miles) after turning into Pulau Carey is **Kampung Sungai Bum-**
bon ❶, home to the Mah Meri (pronounced 'hma meri') Orang Asli people, one of the two indigenous tribes in Peninsular Malaysia who are traditional woodcarvers. Like all traditional Orang Asli, the Mah Meri are animists who worship spirits and conduct ancient ancestral ceremonies. With modern education and influences from the external world, they now speak the Bahasa Malaysia language and many now work in plantations and in the cities. However, the beauty of their heritage lives on in their intricate, unique spirit masks and sculptures.

Dream Designs

Traditionally, woodcarving designs are first revealed to craftsmen in their dreams. Today's carvers use old works as reference, or consult a tome on Mah Meri culture that was put together by a German researcher years ago, which documents the different types of masks and sculptures with photographs. Interestingly, the book also doubles as a sales catalogue, as the carvings are also available for sale. Preservationists fear that tourism and commercialism may con-

Members of the Mah Meri tribe perform a traditional dance

taminate the delicate Mah Meri culture, but some feel this could be the only way the woodcarving tradition can live on.

In the exhibition centre (free) are fine examples of the finished product. A trademark Mah Meri sculpture is the *Muyang Tenong Jerat Harimau*, a monkey and chain ensemble. 'Muyang' is the Mah Meri term for 'spirit', of which there are reputedly over 100.

Carvers are traditionally men, while the women do the finishing, but this is slowly changing. Meanwhile, the women have revived the nearly extinct art of weaving, and their products are also on sale.

For lunch or dinner, return to the bridge. To the right of the bridge on the mainland side is a good eatery, the **Kang Guan Restaurant** (see ❶).

for the mausoleum and mosque, make sure your arms and legs are covered. The sprawling **Istana Bandar Palace** was built by Sultan Abdul Samad's son, Sultan Alauddin Sulaiman Shah.

JUGRA

Head south and right at Jalan Pusara. Enjoy the dive through idyllic rural villages en route to **Jugra** ❷, an old capital of Selangor. All that is left from the glory days are a mausoleum and two historical buildings from the early 20th century, a mosque and palace (daily 9am–5pm; free). You need written permission to enter these (tel: 03-3180 3694) but you may be able to convince the caretaker to let you in;

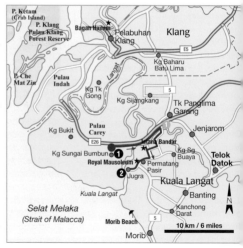

Dataran Putra

PUTRAJAYA

A tribute to Malaysia's period of plenty, the administrative capital of Putrajaya is astounding for the size of its public buildings, monuments and spaces. It looks best when lit up at night.

DISTANCE: Putrajaya is 25km (15.5 miles) south of KL; the route itself covers 41/2km (23/4 miles)
TIME: Half a day
START: Mercu Tanda
END: Taman Botani
POINTS TO NOTE: Start in the late afternoon so you see Putrajaya at night when it looks best. Take the KLIA Transit (20 minutes) from KL Sentral. From the station, hop onto any Nadi Putra bus; all buses from the station go to the attractions featured in this route. The most convenient way around, though, is to hire a taxi (RM30 per hour), while the fit will enjoy a cycling tour (see page 131).

Conceived in the 1990s by then Prime Minister Mahathir Mohamad as his mega pièce de résistance, **Putrajaya** embodies the huge aspirations – literally – of a nation drunk on a decade of year-on-year 10 percent GNP growth rates. Named after the country's first prime minister, Tunku Abdul Rahman Putra al-Haj, and covering 4,900ha (12,200 acres), Putra-

jaya impacts with the sheer scale of its government buildings, public spaces and bridges. Inevitably, it has plenty of detractors, who criticise its lavishness. Others decry its claims to a Muslim heritage, pointing out that the result is more Middle Eastern than local Malay.

PRECINCT 1

On the other hand, however, Putrajaya is a brilliant showcase of postmodern architecture and urban planning. Its centrepiece is **Presint 1** (Precinct 1), from which the rest of the capital radiates. At the heart of Presint 1 is a hill, around which are government offices and the largest artificial wetlands in the tropics. On the hill sits the **Mercu Tanda** ❶ (Putrajaya Landmark), a steel sculpture that symbolises the city's beginnings and contains a time capsule. The sculpture stands among gazebos and fountains in a park, the **Taman Putra Perdana** (Mon–Fri 7am–8pm, Sat, Sun and public holidays 7am–10pm; free).

From this point extends a 4.2-km (2.6-mile) long boulevard, **Persiaran Per-**

Masjid Tuanku Mizan Abdul Zainal

dana, which is the city's spine that links four squares and two bridges.

DATARAN PUTRA

From Taman Putra Perdana, get onto the one-way road that loops around the hill, Persiaran Sultan Salahuddin Abdul Aziz Shah. Head towards **Perdana Putra ❷**, home of the offices of the Prime Minister of Malaysia.

Turn left before Perdana Putra at a sign that points to **Dataran Putra ❸**. This square is actually a circular space with a star-shaped centre-piece, which represents the country's states, while the circle symbolises unity. This is where you get the best view of the green-roofed Perdana Putra. Built in French palatial style, it has an onion-shaped main dome adorned with glazed mosaic, a replica of that of Masjid Zahir, an important mosque in the northern state of Kedah.

PUTRA BRIDGE

Walk down to the **Putra Bridge ❹**. The 435-metre (1,430-ft) bridge, with decorative arches and pavilions, was inspired by the

well-known 17th-century Khaju Bridge in Isfahan, Iran.

PUTRAJAYA LAKE

Turn back to the square, keeping to the left. Look out for stairs leading down to the air-conditioned Selera Putra food court with a view where you can have a drink and a snack or a spicy meal at **Hameed's Nasi Kandar** (see ❶). This is also where you find the jetty for **Cruise**

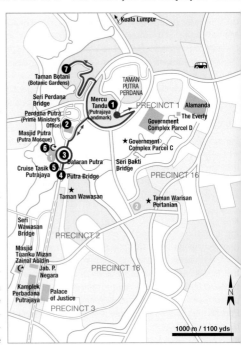

Palace of Justice   *Moroccan Pavilion*

Tasik Putrajaya ❺ (tel: 03-8888 5539; www.cruisetasikputrajaya.com; be there 30 minutes before the ride; rides will be cancelled in heavy rain), which offers 25-minute rides on traditional boats (daily 11am–6.30pm) or 45-minute cruise boat rides (departures 11am–7.45pm) on **Tasik Putrajaya** (Putrajaya Lake). The sunset and night cruises are particularly pretty.

PUTRA MOSQUE

Go back up to the square to visit the **Masjid Putra** ❻ (Putra Mosque; tel: 03-8888 5678; Sat–Thu 9am–noon, 2–4pm, 5–6pm, Fri 2–4pm, 5–6pm; free). The mosque features 16th to 18th-century Persian Islamic architecture, with rose-tinted granite mosaic as tile decorations. Its main entrance is fashioned after public gates in Muslim Persia. Three-quarters of the mosque extends out onto the lake, so it looks like it is 'floating' on water.

POST-MODERN ARCHITECTURE

If you are interested in postmodern architecture, head next to Presint 3.3km (2 miles) over the Putra Bridge. Look out for the Mughal-influenced features of the Istana Kehakiman (Palace of Justice), which faces the gorgeous contemporary Islamic gateway of the Kompleks Perbadanan Putrajaya (Putrajaya Corporation Complex), and the space-age all-steel Masjid Tuanku Mizan Abdul Zainal.

BOTANICAL GARDENS

Otherwise, get back onto Persiaran Sultan Salahudin Abdul Aziz Shah. About 1.5km (1 mile) on is the turn-off to **Taman Botani** ❼ (Botanical Gardens; tel: 03-8888 9090; daily 9am–7pm; charge for some attractions). Stroll, cycle or take a tram ride through its diverse botanical collections, which includes a lovely Sun Garden with a sundial. The elaborate Moroccan Pavilion features replicas of architecture found in four historical Moroccan cities. End the day with a tasty satay dinner at the famous **Sate Kajang Hj Samuri** in Presint 16 (see ❷).

DIRECTORY

Hand-picked hotels and restaurants to suit all budgets and tastes, organised by area, plus select nightlife listings, an alphabetical listing of practical information, a language guide and an overview of the best books and films to give you a flavour of the city.

Double bedroom at the Majestic

ACCOMMODATION

Tourist accommodation in KL includes international brands, home-grown chains, business hotels, boutique establishments as well as serviced apartments and trendy backpacker outfits. Hotels are rated 1 to 5 stars according to international criteria such as size, facilities and staff-to-guest ratio (see the Malaysian Association of Hotels website at www.hotels.org.my). There is a healthy choice of backpackers or flashpackers in the Petaling Street vicinity, which are generally creative conversions of pre-war shophouses; their air-conditioned en suite single/double rooms make sense if you're looking for budget accommodation that is a step up from backpackers. However, light sleepers should check how good the sound-proofing is.

In terms of service, other than the 5-star hotels and backpacker outfits, service can be wanting due to poor training of migrant workers who are widely employed and who have a poor command of English. Be patient.

By law, prices quoted must be nett, inclusive of 6% GST and 10% service taxes. Bargain for better rates, especially for longer stays. Internet and weekend rates in the city tend to be lower. Buffet breakfast is usually included as is Wi-fi, although Wi-fi might not be the best unless it's a five-star hotel or backpackers. Airport transfers and tours are sometimes thrown in.

During peak periods, rooms can be booked out or a steep surcharge imposed. These periods fall on long weekends, Malaysian and Singaporean school holidays, the Formula 1 Grand Prix season in October, public holidays, (especially Chinese New Year, Hari Raya Aidilfitri and Deepavali), and July–August, when Arab tourists flock to the country.

Check in is usually at 2pm, sometimes 3pm and hotels can often be quite hard-nosed about it. However, most allow you to leave your luggage with them for free, before you check in and after you check out.

Historic Heart

Avenue J Hotel

13, Leboh Pasar Besar; tel: 03-2022 3338; http://avenuejhotels.com; $$

Unbeatable views of the colonial quarter are to be had from the upper floors of the Avenue J Hotel. Architects did a good job blending this new Edwardian-influenced building with its surround-

---

Price for a double room with breakfast and taxes:
$$$$ = ver RM550
$$$ = RM350–549
$$ = RM150–349
$ = below RM150

Bathroom at the Majestic

ings. Rooms are small but the beds are comfortable and the hand-drawn wall art is a nice personal touch.

Majestic Hotel

5 Jalan Sultan Hishamuddin; tel: 03-2785 8000; www.majestickl.com; $$$$

Comprising a restored wing of the colonial-era hotel of the same name, the Majestic is luxurious and offers service to match. The decor is beautiful with touches like the orchid-filled conservatory, and the on-site Cantango Restaurant is excellent.

Petaling Street and Surroundings

1000 Miles

17 & 19 Jalan Tun H S Lee; tel: 03-2022 3333; http://1000mileskl.com; $

Centrally located, this budget hotel has helpful staff and rooms that are sparse but very clean; en suites are available but note that rooms with windows can be a little noisy. Night-time is great to spend on the roof patio.

Back Home

30 Jalan Tun H.S. Lee; tel: 03-2022 0788; www.backhome.com.my; $

This thoughtfully-renovated backpackers' guesthouse spreads across a row of shophouses within walking distance to Petaling Street. Beds are comfy and have partitions for privacy. All rooms have washbasins and there is also a female-only dorm. A nice touch is an open-air chilling-out section.

Explorers Guest House

128 & 130 Jalan Tun H S Lee; tel: 03-2022 2928; www.facebook.com/theexplorers guesthousekl; $

Located opposite the Sin Sze Si Ya Temple, this friendly, cheerful backpackers' guesthouse sits in a four-storey building (no lifts). Private rooms and dorms are available, including a female-only dorm. Wi-fi is free but only available on the ground floor.

Geo Hotel Kuala Lumpur

7 Jalan Hang Kasturi; tel: 03-2032 2288; www.geohotelkl.com; $

This basic, clean hotel is in a terrific location right by the Pasar Seni LRT station and just across from Central Market. Smoking rooms have balconies. Head out for excellent local breakfasts in the vicinity.

Mingle

53 Jalan Sultan; tel: 03-2022 2078; www.minglekl.com; $-$$

Painstakingly-refurbished to maintain the integrity of its century-old shophouse building, this laid-back non-smoking flashpacker hangout offers comfortable rooms and dorms and a great restaurant. There are lots of stairs but they lead to a wonderful roof terrace.

Swiss-Inn Kuala Lumpur

62 Jalan Sultan; tel: 03-2072 3333; www.swissgarden.com; $$

This hotel has held its own for a long time. It fronts a street with Chinese eat-

Double bedroom at the Grand Hyatt

eries and tea shops, while the back of it opens directly onto the Petaling Street Bazaar. Rooms, though basic, are clean and value for money.

Kuala Lumpur City Centre

Ascott Kuala Lumpur

9 Jalan Pinang; tel: 03-2718 6868; www.the-ascott.com; $$$

This serviced apartment across the KLCC has splendid views of the city from its rooftop pool. Options range from studio to three-bedroom apartments, all with fully equipped kitchens and facilities that cater to families and business folk.

Concorde Hotel

2 Jalan Sultan Ismail; tel: 03-2144 2200; http://kualalumpur.concordehotelsresorts. com; $$

Guests enjoy this hotel's large and airy rooms, having the Hard Rock Café next door and the KLCC within walking distance. Guests in the Premier Executive Wing enjoy a range of services, such as complimentary limousine transfers from the airport, free refreshments at the lounge and a separate reception area.

Fraser Place

10 Jalan Perak; tel: 03-2118 6288; http://kualalumpur.frasershospitality.com; $$$

Excellent house-keeping ensures that these generous-sized serviced apartments are in tip-top shape. The fully-equipped kitchens are a pleasure to

use, and there are study areas as well as living and dining rooms.

GTower Hotel

199 Jalan Tun Razak; tel: 03-2168 1919; www.gtowerhotel.com; $$$

Ultra-modern and stylish, this business hotel is a green building with great sky-line views from its upper-floor pool, bars and restaurants. It has one of the best gyms in town, but unfortunately is not child-friendly.

Grand Hyatt

12 Jalan Pinang; tel: 03-2182 1234; http://kualalumpur.grand.hyatt.com; $$$$

Floor-to-ceiling windows afford tremendous views of the KLCC from well-appointed rooms. The service is uniformly impeccable and it has a gorgeous restaurant/bar, a saltwater swimming pool and a well-equipped gym.

Impiana KLCC Hotel

13 Jalan Pinang; tel: 03-2147 1111; http://kualalumpurhotels.impiana.com. my; $$

This retreat for business travellers offers spacious, modern rooms, a wide choice of therapies at the highly-regarded Swasana Spa and a lovely infinity pool. Club facilities are good and worth the extra cost.

Mandarin Oriental

Kuala Lumpur City Centre; tel: 03-2380 8888; www.mandarinoriental.com/ kualalumpur; $$$$

Suite at the Traders Hotel

Located right next to the Petronas Twin Towers, this luxury hotel has large guest rooms that combine traditional and contemporary furnishings with cutting-edge technology. The ceiling-to-floor windows offer premium views of the KLCC and the inside is uplifted by 300-odd original artworks displayed throughout the hotel.

Renaissance Hotel
Corner Jalan Sultan Ismail/Jalan Ampang; tel: 03-2162 2233; www.marriott.com; $$$
Newly refurbished rooms imbue this Mariott Hotel with a fresh, contemporary feel, with the upper floor rooms in the east wing having the best views. The breakfast here is great and key attractions and public transport links are close by.

Shangri-La Hotel
11 Jalan Sultan Ismail; tel: 03-2032 2388; www.shangri-la.com/kualalumpur/shangrila; $$$
Lovely gardens, a large gym and capacious rooms are the hallmarks of this hotel. The restaurants are popular at weekends, so book a table if you are dining there. The KL Tower and the lush Bukit Nanas Forest Reserve are just behind.

Traders Hotel
Kuala Lumpur City Centre; tel: 03-2332 9888; www.shangri-la.com/kualalumpur/traders; $$$
Connected to the KL Convention Centre, this sleek hotel is popular with business travellers, with five exclusive Traders Club floors. The contemporary-style rooms have full-length windows with views of either the city or the Twin Towers. Its poolside bar is the hottest hangout in town.

Villa Samadhi
8, Pesiaran Madge; tel: 03-9212 0372; www.villasamadhi.com.my; $$$$
A tropical retreat in the diplomatic quarter about 3km (1.75 miles) east of the KLCC, this luxurious boutique hotel serves up charm and quiet in the shape of wooden villas surrounded by lush greenery. It is a place to relax and unwind.

KL Sentral, Brickfields and Mid Valley

Boulevard-St Giles Premier Hotel
Mid Valley City, Lingkaran Syed Putra; tel: 03-2295 8000; www.stgiles.com; $$
The Mid Valley area has two enormous malls, so this hotel is great for shoppers. The rooms are large and the staff, well-trained. It provides a shuttle to the Bangsar LRT station, and the KTM Komuter train station is within walking distance.

The Gardens Hotel & Residences
Mid Valley City, Lingkaran Syed Putra; tel: 03-2268 1188; www.stgiles.com; $$$
The more upmarket sister hotel to the Boulevard, this is also located within

Hilton Kuala Lumpur swimming pool

the dual-shopping mall complex, and will appeal to shoppers. The rooms are clean and airy and there are also apartment options.

Hilton Kuala Lumpur

3 Jalan Stesen Sentral; tel: 03-2264 2264; www.kuala-lumpur.hilton.com; $$$

Directly across from KL Sentral, this hotel's bright rooms have floor-to-ceiling windows with views of the city, luxurious beds, rain showers and large-screen plasma TVs. A free-form pool, a swanky multi-restaurant hub and the cool Zeta Bar add to its appeal.

PODs the Backpackers Home

6-1, No 30 Jalan Thambipillay; tel: 03-2276 0858; http://podsbackpacker.com; $

A fun outfit with rooms and dorms, including a female-only dorm, this hostel offers free breakfast and can arrange tours and bus tickets for you. It is within walking distance of KL Sentral, which also makes it a great place to shower and rest before a journey.

Signature Hotel Little India

130E Jalan Thamby Abdullah; tel: 03-2272 4435; http://littleindia.mysignaturehotel.com.my; $

The colours of this hotel, located on the edge of Brickfields, are as bright and chirpy as the service and rooms. While small, the rooms are adequate, modern and clean. Quality eateries abound nearby. Don't mistake this for the lesser sister hotel on Jalan Thambipillay.

North of Masjid India

The Reeds Boutique Hotel

9 Jalan Yap Ah Shak; tel: 03-2602 0330; http://thereedshotel.com; $

Set a little away from the tourist areas north of Masjid India, this budget hotel, with a hipster twist, offers smoke-free rooms and dorms in a heritage building. A short-walk away are a selection of good eateries and the nightlife scene at The Row.

Sheraton Imperial

Jalan Sultan Ismail; tel: 03-2717 9900; www.sheratonimperialkualalumpur.com; $$

With traditional wooden furnishing and spacious rooms and bathrooms, this hotel offers good service and a comfortable stay. Go for the Club rooms or try asking for a tower view room upgrade to enjoy the twinkling lights of the KL Tower at night.

WP Hotel

362 Jalan Tunku Abdul Rahman; tel: 2618 1188; www.wphotel.com.my; $

A rooftop terrace with a swimming pool and a city skyline view is this two-star outfit's main draw. Rooms are comfortable – higher floors are quieter – and the Wi-fi is good, even by the pool. Great food close by, including famous Kampung Baru eats.

Bukit Bintang

Anggun Boutique Hotel

7 & 9 Tengkat Tong Shin; tel: 03-2145 8003; www.anggunkl.com; $$

Room at The Ritz–Carlton

Lovely Malay architectural influences are the calling card of this hotel, including a rustic internal courtyard. Rooms are plush and those with balconies overlook the bustling street; courtyard-facing rooms on upper floors are quieter.

Chaos Hotel

Lot B-1, Fahrenheit 88, 179 Jalan Bukit Bintang; tel: 03-2148 6688; www.chaoshotel.com; $$

A project by design company Chaos Lab, this minimalist gem is located in the back section of a mall, smack in the middle of the Bukit Bintang shopping area. The beds are all comfortable but go for the larger rooms.

Invito Hotel Suites

1 Lorong Ceylon, Bukit Ceylon; tel: 03-2386 9288; www.invitohotelsuites.com.my; $$$

Set a little away from the Changkat hub, these contemporary well-appointed apartments have great beds, fully equipped kitchens and excellent Wi-fi. Step out into the balcony to enjoy views of the city. Monorail stations are within walking distance.

JW Marriott

183 Jalan Bukit Bintang; tel: 03-2715 9000; www.marriott.com; $$$$

Recently renovated, this hotel has all the required mod cons for travellers. It is part of the Starhill Gallery complex, so guests can take advantage of the spa and health facilities in the mall

and charge their dining expenses at the Feast Village to their rooms.

Paper Plane Hostel

15 Jalan Sin Chew Kee; tel: 03- 2110 1676; www.paperplanehostel.com; $

Set in a quiet neighbourhood close to the main Bukit Bintang action, this stylish backpackers' guesthouse, complete with funky art on the walls, offers clean dorms and rooms and friendly service. There aren't many communal areas, but there are cafés are close by.

Parkroyal

Jalan Sultan Ismail; tel: 03 2147 0088; www.parkroyalhotels.com; $$

Located along the shopping strip and close to great Jalan Imbi street food, this hotel continues to offer good service, with an outstanding buffet breakfast. For great views, go for an upper floor room.

The Ritz-Carlton

168 Jalan Imbi; tel: 03-2142 8000; www.ritzcarlton.com; $$$$

This has one of the city's best personalised butler services with service overall paying nice attention to details. Indulge in luxurious spa baths and therapies at its Spa Village. A covered walkway links to the Starhill Gallery, and from there to other malls.

Sarang Vacation Homes

4 Jalan Sin Chew Kee, tel: 012-333 5666; 012-2100218 (mobile), www.sarangvacationhomes.com. $

First World Hotel at Genting Highlands Resort

Enjoy a Malaysian home experience in these houses, which date back to the 1920s. Available for rent as rooms or in their entirety, the houses are homey, comfortable and friendly. A minimum 2-night stay is required during peak periods.

Twenty 5 by Ohana

Taragon Puteri Bintang, Jalan Changkat Thambi Dollah; tel: 012-695 6608; www.ohana-suite.com/twenty5; $

A backpackers' hangout with a view like this one is hard to beat. Located on the 25th floor behind Berjaya Times Square, you can chill on the balcony, cook in the huge kitchen and hang out in the lounge. Rooms and dorms are available, including a female-only dorm. Guests can also use the building's swimming pool and gym.

WOLO Bukit Bintang

Corner of Jalan Bukit Bintang and Jalan Sultan Ismail; tel: 03-2719 1333; www.thewolo.com; $$

The WOLO works hard to embody the 'We Only Live Once' spirit with edgy, contemporary design and statement-making artwork throughout the hotel. Literally in the heart of Bukit Bintang yet well sound-proofed, it offers stylish rooms with tatami beds and a few surprises.

Fraser's Hill
Stephen's Place

Buona Vista, Jalan Peninjau; tel: 013-818 5760; www.facebook.com/pages/Stephens-Place/1536048509948644; $$

Nature lovers will enjoy this charming B&B run by a wildlife photographer who lets out four rooms in a 1930s bungalow of which he is custodian. No Internet but loads of birds, moths and other forest critters big and small.

The Smokehouse Hotel & Restaurant

Jalan Jeriau; tel: 09-362 2226; www.thesmokehouse.com.my; $$$

Built in 1924, this Tudor-style gem has beautiful stone masonry and manicured gardens. It is rather run-down but the rooms are cosy, and each one is different, offering either hill or garden views. The public spaces are filled with chintz and memorabilia.

Genting Highlands
Genting Highlands Resort

Tel: 03-2718 1118; www.rwgenting.com/hotel/accommodation; $–$$$$

Choose from various hotels with over 10,000 rooms on Genting Highlands: the 5-star Genting Grand Hotel and Maxims (where the casino is); the 4-star Resort Hotel; the budget First World Hotel (said to be the world's largest hotel and where the indoor theme park is); and the 2-star Awana Hotel, near Gohtong Jaya.

Kuala Selangor
Grand Kapar Hotel Kuala Selangor

41 Jalan Melati 3/17, Bandar Malawati; tel: 03-3289 2255; $

Right by the bus station is a clean, friendly budget hotel with air-conditioning and hot water that is surrounded

Swimming pool at the Hilton Petaling Jaya

by eateries. It is a little away from Bukit Melawati but the hotel can arrange taxis.

Kuala Selangor Nature Park
Jalan Klinik; tel: 03-3289 2294; $

Accommodation options are basic room-only A-frame huts (twin-share) and chalets (triple-share) with attached bathrooms. Amenities include running water, 24-hour electricity and a common kitchen, but not much else. Walk 10 minutes to the old town centre for meals.

Petaling Jaya

Hilton Petaling Jaya
2 Jalan Barat; tel: 03-7955 9122; www.hilton.com; $$

Located just off the Federal Highway, this established hotel has airy rooms, delicious local cuisine and a popular pub that serves excellent steaks. The gym is good for fitness buffs and the spa next to it does wonders for muscle soreness afterwards.

Project Uchi
65 Jalan SS 2/6, Taman Bahagia; tel: 017-3788 303; www.projectuchi.com; $

Get a real feel of the suburbs in this dorm-only backpackers' guesthouse, located in a terraced house and run by a mother-and-daughter team. The LRT is close by, as are local shops and eateries and a great night market.

Sunway Resort Hotel & Spa
Persiaran Lagoon, Bandar Sunway; tel: 03-7492 8000; www.sunwayhotels.com; $$$

A family-friendly hotel with easy access to the Sunway Lagoon Water theme park and Sunway Pyramid shopping mall. The decor is a kitschy Malaysian version of South Africa's famous Palace of the Lost City at Sun City. Avoid rooms just beneath the lobby as it can be noisy overhead.

Putrajaya/Sepang

The Everly Putrajaya
1 Jalan Alamanda 2, Precint 1; tel: 03-8892 2929; http://putrajaya.theeverlyhotel.com; $$

Right next to the Alamanda shopping centre and with rooms overlooking the lake, this hotel has large comfortable rooms and restaurants with great service. The peaceful yet convenient location draws weekenders.

Sama-sama Hotel KLIA
Jalan Cta 4b, KLIA; tel: 03-8787 3333; www.samasamahotels.com; $$$

This airport hotel is 5 minutes' walk from the terminal. The staff here are friendly and experienced in handling grumpy passengers. The rooms are well-appointed and the spa and swimming pool, great stress-busters.

Sama-sama Express
Mezanine Level, Satellite A Building, KLIA; tel: 03-8787 4848; Level 3, Satellite Building, KLIA2; tel: 03- 8775 6600; www.samasamaexpress.com; $$

Conveniently located within both airports, this transit hotel chain is a great place for even a short layover. Grab a hot shower or a snooze where you can stretch out.

Contango Restaurant

RESTAURANTS

Malaysians love eating, so food is available around the clock. Some street or hawker food centres, Indian Muslim *mamak* eateries and several fast-food chains never close, especially in busy tourist areas. If in doubt about the freshness of the food, ask when the last top-up was done. Locals will swear that hawker food is the best food on earth. How to choose what to eat? Read up about it on the many, quality Malaysian food blogs or ask locals; otherwise, be adventurous, just follow the crowd and order from stalls that attract the most custom. Alternatively, food tours are a great option. Hawker stall dining, whether in a *kopitiam* (coffee shop) or exposed to the elements on a roadside kerb, is an experience in itself. Incidentally, you pay when the food and drinks arrive at your table.

Restaurants tend to close on Mondays but eateries in malls follow mall hours. Last orders are taken half an hour or more before closing time.

Chopsticks are used in Chinese eateries, but you can ask for a plate and cutlery, which translates in Malaysia to a fork and spoon, no knives. Patrons of Malay and Indian eateries often use their hands to eat but again, forks and spoons are readily available too.

Double-check if 'fresh fruit juice' is freshly squeezed or comes in a bottle. Alcohol is very expensive, so take advantage of happy hour or drink at local *kopitiam*. Cocktails can be interesting, with occasional additions of local ingredients such as *gula melaka* palm sugar and local fruit. All restaurants impose a 6% GST charge but they don't all impose a 10% service fee, so tip if you enjoyed good service – just leave the money on the table. Except for very expensive restaurants, Malaysians don't dress up for dinner.

Historic Heart

Contango

Majestic Hotel, 5 Jalan Sultan Hishamuddin; tel: 03-2785 8000; www.majestickl.com; daily 10am–9pm; $$$$

A wide variety of Asian and Continental food is on offer for breakfast, lunch and dinner at this buffet-only restaurant. From wood-oven pizzas and sushi to chilly crab and Mongolian BBQ, leave room for the astonishing desserts. It also boasts a 2,000- bottle capacity wine cellar.

Precious Old China Restaurant & Bar

Lot 2, Mezzanine Floor, Central Market, Jalan Hang Kasturi; tel: 03-2273 7372; www.old

> Price per person for a three-course meal without drinks:
> $$$$ = over RM100
> $$$ = RM70–100
> $$ = RM30–70
> $ = below RM30

Biryani

china.com.my; daily 11.30am–9.30pm; $$
Eclectically decorated with Victorian furniture and antique Chinese wall panels, this restaurant's draws are its chicken, cooked *pongteh* or devilled-style, omelette with *cincalok* (fermented prawns), and the fried *asam* prawns and *lemak nenas* squid. End with a creamy *bubur cha-cha* dessert.

Petaling Street

Einstein's Café
58 Jalan Sultan; tel: 012-363 6004; www.facebook.com/einstein.cafe.kl; Tue–Sun 10am–9pm; $
Located on the 1st floor above an opticians, this laid-back, hip outfit dishes up tasty vegetarian food and great lattes and milkshakes. Try its pizza on a roti or burger and fries. Local options are also available. It's very busy at lunch.

Hong Ngek Restaurant
50 Jalan Tun H.S. Lee; tel: 03-2078 7852; Mon–Sat 11am–7pm; $
Tuck into deep-fried pork ribs, pomfret in two styles (steamed and deep-fried), and double-boiled winter melon soup. Its Hokkien noodles are also a must – yellow noodles in a sticky dark sauce with pork, seafood and vegetables.

Moontree House
6 Jalan Panggung; tel: 03-2031 0537; http://moontree-house.blogspot.my; Wed–Mon 10am–8pm; $
This is a quiet oasis for lovingly-brewed java and flower tea, together with quality cakes and pastries – the home-made cheesecake is a winner. Perched on the 1st floor of a pre-war shophouse, it is also part store, mostly of Mandarin feminist books and handicraft by women artists. LGBT friendly.

Water Lily Vegetarian Restaurant
23 Jalan Tun H S Lee; tel: 03-2070 6561; daily 10am–3pm, 5–9.30pm; $
This no-frills eatery dishes up tasty home-cooked Chinese vegetarian dishes using mock meats, leafy greens and mushrooms. There are value-for-money set meals of boiled rice with two dishes. Otherwise, try the ginger duck noodles or stir-fried vermicelli.

Kuala Lumpur City Centre

Al-Rawsha
8 Jalan Kampung Pandan; tel: 03-9200 6600; www.alrawshakl.com; daily 24 hours; $$
Housed in a huge castle-like structure near the TREC entertainment hub, this Lebanese restaurant dishes up a range of eats, including Kofta geills and Yemeni rice dishes, including Lamb Mandy and Kabsah. It is a favourite with tour groups so it gets busy.

Bombay Palace
Life Centre, M-3A, Mezzanine Floor, 20 Jalan Sultan Ismail; tel: 03-2171 7220; daily noon–2.30pm and 6.30–10.30pm; $$$
Fine North Indian cuisine, a classy environment and attentive service make for a great dining experience. Go for a balcony table overlooking the street. The grills are

exceptional (a smoky experience though); other must-tries are the fish masala and chicken makhani. The naans and chaats (savouries) are other stand-outs.

Dharma Realm Guan Yin Sagely Monastery

161 Jalan Ampang; tel: 03-2164 8055; Mon–Fri 11am–4pm; $

Queue up with other vegans for a Chinese 'Buddhist' buffet in the simple canteen of the monastery. The canteen serves a large variety of hot food, salads and fruit. Meals are served free on the auspicious 1st and 15th days of the month of the lunar calendar.

Fuego

Level 23a, Tower B, The Troika, 19 Persiaran KLCC; tel: 03-2162 0886; daily 6.30–11pm (drinks until 1am); $$$$

One of the hottest restaurants in town with a great view of the skyline, start with a pre-dinner cocktail with a twist, then go on to dinner, which draws from Mexican and South American traditions, so it features tapas, guacamole and grills. Note that reservations are a must and there are two seatings.

Hakka Restaurant

6 Jalan Kia Peng; tel: 03-2143 1908; daily noon–3pm and 6–11.30pm; $$

This family-run restaurant, over 40 years old, is the best place for authentic Hakka food. Must-tries are the Hakka noodles with minced pork sauce, *mui choy kau yok* (braised pork belly layered with preserved vegetables) and the tender *yim kok kai* (salt-baked chicken).

Hale Restaurant

Lot 1-20 First Floor, Menara Hap Seng, Jalan P Ramlee; tel: 012-658 8020; www.halerestaurant.com; Mon–Fri 7.30am– 8pm, Sat 8am–3pm; $

Healthy fast food that is affordable and tasty is what this new outfit offers in the shape of wholemeal burgers, tortilla wraps and salads, all made in-house. Have these with a cold-pressed juice, home-made lemongrass tea or organic coffee.

Restaurant Lafite

Shangri-La Hotel, 11 Jalan Sultan Ismail; tel: 03-2074 3900; Mon–Fri noon–2.30pm, Mon–Sat 7–10.30pm; $$$$

This French restaurant has been on the map for a long time but it retains its reputation through exquisite preparation and presentation, particularly its beautifully crafted desserts. Opt for the set if you want to try a bit of everything. The dress code is smart casual.

Limapulo

The Row, 26 Jalan Doraisamy; tel: 03-2698 3268; Mon–Sat noon-3pm, 6–10pm; www.facebook.com/pages/Baba-Can-Cook/635621076504974; $

Delicious and cheap set lunches are the highlight of this restaurant. Noodle-lovers will enjoy the *mee siam* and *nonya laksa* and rice-lovers, the *ayam berempah* creamy curry chicken with boiled

Shang Palace

rice. The old-school setting is charming and the owner is often around to make sure all's well.

Little Penang Kafe

Lot 409–411, 4/F, Suria KLCC; tel: 03-2163 0215; daily 10am–10pm; $

Serves dishes from the island of Penang, well known as a gourmet paradise. Try the *char kway teow* (fried flat rice noodles), hot and sour *asam laksa* with a spicy tamarind fish gravy, and Hokkien prawn noodles. For dessert, order *ice kacang*, a sweet shaved ice treat. There is a branch at Mid Valley Megamall (tel: 03-2282 0215).

Peter Hoe Café

56-1, First Floor, The Row, 26 Jalan Doraisamy; tel: 012-334 7123; www.face book.com/Peterhoecafe; daily, 11.30am–5.30pm; $$

Order tasty treats, including healthy signature quiches, pastas, soups and salads from a Western menu with Eastern twists, which varies from week to week. Lamb and beef are served on weekends. It has a comfortable, airy atmosphere in a contemporary setup and links to its excellent gift shop.

Pier 12 Seafood Tavern

Old Malaya, 66 Jalan Raja Chulan; tel: 011-2611 2460; www.facebook.com/pg/pier12old malaya; daily noon–3pm and 5pm–1am; $$$$

From a great location at the end of the charming Old Malaya lot, this place offers an eyeful of the KL Tower from the upstairs patio as you enjoy happy-hour mojitos and margaritas (12–9pm), or feast on garlic prawn and mini squid starters. A must-try main is the tandoori halibut.

Salad Atelier

Lot G-09A, G/F, The Weld, 76 Jalan Raja Chulan; tel: 017-415 6269; www.saladatelier. com; Mon–Fri 7.30am–9.30am, 11am–9pm, Sat 10am–6pm; $

Mix and match fresh ingredients to make your own salads and sandwiches at this healthy, chirpy outlet. Choose from greens, meat, cheese and fruit and wash it down with fresh juice. It also has outlet at Avenue K and the Intermark.

Shang Palace

Shangri-la Hotel, 11 Jalan Sultan Ismail; tel: 03-2074 3904; www.shangri-la.com/ kualalumpur/shangrila; daily noon–2.30pm and 6.30–10.30pm, opens at 10.30am on Sun and public holidays; $$$$

Famous for its Peking duck, the Shang Palace also offers other Cantonese staples such as dried seafood, steamed fish, crispy chicken in salt and stewed and fried noodles. Vegetarians will be happy with its many available options.

Tamarind Hill

19A Jalan Sultan Ismail; tel: 03-2148 3200; Mon–Fri noon–3pm, daily 6pm–midnight; $$$$

A gorgeous wood, water and thatch setting for the romantic at heart, this Thai-Burmese restaurant makes you feel

Fried noodles

pampered. Salty, sour, spicy and sweet are beautifully balanced and the presentation exquisite. Wines, cocktails and alcoholic drinks are available here; otherwise the lemon grass drink is delightfully refreshing.

Trattoria Il Porcellino

G/F, Menara Hap Seng, Jalan P Ramlee; tel: 03-2022 0460; www.trattoriaasia.com; Mon–Fri 8am–midnight, Sat 10am–11pm; $$$

Start off with parma ham and mortadella cold cuts, follow up with a pie-like pizza or homemade pasta. For a lighter option, try the ciabatta. This is a laid-back eatery with outdoor seating and air-conditioned tables.

Zenzero Restaurant and Wine Bar

A-0-9 G/F, St Mary Place, 1 Jalan Tengah; tel: 03-2022 3883; ww.zenzero.com.my; Sun–Fri noon–late, Sat 6pm–late; $$$$

This Italian restaurant exudes an elegant yet cosy ambience: try the eggplant ravioli, Black Angus beef, grilled or braised, or lobster linguini. It also has a good wine list as well as classic Italian and house cocktails. If you're there for lunch, the express lunch menu is good value.

Bangsar

Agak-Agak

APW, 29 Jalan Riong; tel: 03-2201 3650; www.agakagakinitiative.com; Tue–Sat 10am–6pm; $$$

An eatery with a difference á la Jamie Oliver's Fifteen programme, whose apprentice cooks come from marginal-ised backgrounds and are being honed by celebrity chefs for a career in the food industry. The menu is Malaysian with a twist.

Alexis Bangsar

29 Jalan Telawi 3, Bangsar Baru; tel: 03-2284 2880; www.alexis.com.my; daily 10am–midnight; $$

Famous for its spicy Sarawak *laksa* noodles, this smart, casual dining restaurant also serves good Neapolitan and margherita pizzas, and fish and chips. It has a bar with live music upstairs and branches in the Bangsar Shopping Centre, Mid-Valley Megamall and on Jalan Ampang.

A Li Yaa

48 G&M, Medan Setia 2, Bukit Damansara; 03-2092 5378; http://aliyaa.com; 11am–11pm; $$$$

Curried crab cooked in traditional Jaffna style is the star dish of this classy Sri Lankan restaurant. Other must-tries include the bone marrow masala, Ceylon devilled prawns and traditional Kiribath rice cakes. End your meal with a fluffy sweet *apam*. The restaurant is located in a quiet enclave away from the main Bangsar strips.

Basil Thai Nudle Bar

G10, G/F, Bangsar Village, 1 Jalan Telawi 1; tel: 03-2287 8708; daily noon–10pm; $$

This is a casual café with a menu of traditional Thai dishes. The special mixed combo platter, with spring rolls, *wan tons* and fish cakes, is an appe-

tite-whetting starter. For mains, order the prawn *tom yam* (hot and sour soup), green curry or stir-fried beef with basil.

Cava Restaurant and Bar

71 Jalan Bangkung; tel: 03-2093 6637; daily noon–3pm and 6–midnight; http://cava.my/v2; $$$$

Good Spanish staples on offer include paella and baked fish, together with tapas and Spanish cheeses. For a Malaysian twist, try the lemongrass infused pasta or *patatas bravas* with cili padi pesto. Their wine list is extensive and it's got a great ambience for a romantic date night.

Pulp by Papa Palheta

APW, 29 Jalan Riong; tel: 03-2201 3650; www.pulpcoffee.co; Mon–Fri 7.30am–10pm, Sat–Sun 9am–11pm; $$$

Unless you're a seriously serious coffee drinker, this boutique café is probably not for you. With rotating and modular coffee bars as well as a host of specialty equipment, baristas will make you carefully-sourced coffee exactly the way you want it. Salads and sandwiches are also available.

Brickfields

Analakshmi

Temple of Fine Arts, 112 Jalan Berhala; tel: 03-2274 3709; www.tfa.org.my; Tue–Sun 11.30am–3pm, 6.30–10pm; $

Prepared by the centre's volunteers, fine South Indian vegetarian food is on offer; proceeds go back to the centre. Most diners opt for the buffet, with the weekend spreads the largest; if you choose á la carte, you pay whatever you like. Dress code applies.

Indian Spices Village

204 Jalan Tun Sambanthan; tel: 03-2276 6484; 8.30am–11pm; $

A generous, cheap *thali* set of rice, vegetables and meats and yoghurt, makes this eatery a popular choice. Its South Indian offerings are better than its North Indian dishes, but make sure you about the daily specials. This is also one of the cleanest eateries in Brickfields.

Peter Pork Noodle

Restoran One Sentral, 7 Jalan Tun Sambanthan 4; daily 7am–2.30pm; $

This single hawker stall is legendary for the quality of its signature dish. Tender minced and sliced pork is cooked with your choice of noodles in a hearty soup and topped with crispy deep-fried lard. Wash it down with an ice-cold drink.

Sin Kee Restoran

194 Jalan Tun Sambanthan; tel: 03-2274 1842; Tue–Sun noon–2.30pm and 6–9.30pm; $

Sample home-style Chinese food by ordering a few dishes to share: *sambal* (chilli paste) prawns, fresh seafood steamed with rice, *fu yung*-style omelette with Chinese sausage, prawns and onions. Hainanese-style one-dish 'West-

ern' meals such as fish and chips, and lamb and chicken chops are available too.

Singh Chapati House
55 Jalan Thambipillay; tel: 03-2272 1215; daily 8am–midnight; $

Punjabi food at its best is on offer here in this humble eatery. As its name indicates, it is the bread you should order, which is freshly-made, soft and thick. A small but very good choice of curries is laid out, and vegetarian options are also available. End your meal with the excellent Punjabi-style masala tea with fresh milk.

Masjid India and surrounds

Em by Ted Boy
Hotel Transit, 42 Jalan Pudu; tel: 03-2022 2056; www.tedboy.com/em; Mon–Sat 10am–10pm; $

This café, with its terrific laid-back atmosphere, serves up wholesome meals and homemade pastries. Highlights are their freshly-baked bagels, hearty breakfasts and 'Mediterranean with a touch of Asian' offerings. It has outlets in Bangsar and elsewhere in KL too.

Lakshmi Vilas
57 Lebuh Ampang; tel: 03-2072 2166; daily 7am–10pm; $

Affordable South Indian vegetarian meals are served in this 50-year-old no-frills eatery. Enjoy hot rice with the fried and curried vegetable dishes of the day on a banana leaf, after which only the hard-nosed would be able to resist a sweet or savoury snack from those on

tantalising display.

Nasi Kandar Ibrahimsha
68 Jalan Tuanku Abdul Rahman; tel: 03-2693 6680; daily 7am–7.30pm; $

It is Penang-style Indian Muslim curries galore here at this oldie-but-goodie. Choose from fish head, squid, beef, lamb and other curries, to be splashed over rice, but the specialty is *ayam masak hitam*, a spicy chicken cooked in a healthy dose of soya sauce.

O'Brien's
G/F, Menara OCBC, 18 Jalan Tun Perak; tel: 03-2698 2281; Mon–Sat 7am–9pm; $

This tiny outlet serves freshly made sandwiches from an eclectic menu with choices like toasted Crambo Club Tootsie with chicken, bacon and cheese. The café also has great gourmet coffee and fresh juices.

Yut Kee
35 Jalan Dang Wangi; tel: 03-2698 8108; Tue–Sun 8am–5pm; $

A Hainanese coffee shop dating from 1928, well known for *roti babi*, a sandwich filled with minced pork and crabmeat, dipped in egg and then deep-fried, served with Worcestershire sauce. Not to be missed too are the *asam* (tamarind) prawns, *belacan* (shrimp paste) fried rice and beef tripe stew.

Kampung Baru

CT Rose
Jalan Datuk Abdul Razak (opposite Sekolah

Three-flavour fish

Kebangsaan Kampung Baru); tel: 016-997 8701; daily 6.30pm–5.30am; $

The biggest *nasi lemak* eatery in the city where locals come to get their fix of coconut rice cooked in giant pots. More pots are filled with different *sambal* (chilli paste) of anchovies, squid, beef *rendang* and chicken curry.

Jalan Raja Muda Musa Hawker Centre

Jalan Raja Muda Musa; daily 6.30am–1am; $

The stalls here are good for Malay specialities such as *lontong* (rice cakes with coconut gravy) and the east coast regional favourite, *nasi kerabu* (herbed rice salad). The selection of home-made *kuih* desserts is terrific. Many of which feature bananas, glutinous rice and coconut, whether grated or cooked with coconut milk.

Restoran Noorizan Gerak Dua Puluh Satu

7, Jalan Raja Muda Musa; 7am–midnight; $

The famous Pak Lang *ikan bakar* at this hawker centre draws long queues, but it is worth waiting for this tasty spicy grilled fish, to be enjoyed with chilly soya sauce.

Restoran Grand Garuda Baru

176 Jalan Raja Abdullah; tel: 03-2202 7170; www.garuda.my; daily 10am–11pm; $

This Indonesian minang restaurant serves traditional West Sumatran *nasi padang* (rice with side dishes). Try the *ayam pop* (deep-fried chicken), crispy beef *dendeng* and the oxtail soup. Wash

it down with *aipokat* (avocado juice). It can be quite chaotic when busy, but that just adds to the atmosphere.

Bukit Bintang

Ben's

6.11.00 & E6.11.00, 6th Floor Pavilion KL Shopping Mall 168 Jalan Bukit Bintang; tel: 03-2141 5290; http://thebiggroup.co/bens; 11am–11pm; $$$

Hipsters adore the restaurants and cafés in the Big Group's stable. Choose from an interesting menu that includes soft shell crab spaghetti, butter chicken and a Thai beef salad. Dine in the chic indoors or sit outdoors for a view of Bukit Bintang, prettily lit up at night.

Din Tai Fong

Lot 6.01.05, 6/F, Pavilion KL, 168 Jalan Bukit Bintang; tel: 03-2148 8292; daily 10am–10pm; $$

Tasty Shanghainese *xiao long pao* and *shaomai* dumplings are what draw the crowds to this Taiwanese global chain restaurant. Hearty chicken and beef soups with noodles are also must-haves. End with a red bean soup dessert. The restaurant is always busy but wait-staff manage well and with a smile.

Enak

Feast Floor, Starhill Gallery; tel: 03-2141 8973; daily noon–midnight; $$$

Malay cuisine is served here in an elegant setting. Try the king prawns simmered in a creamy coconut milk sauce and slow-cooked beef with spices and herbs.

Perdana Botanical Garden

A–Z

A

Addresses

All road signs and place names are in Bahasa Malaysia (Malay) but many also appear in English. In this guidebook we have chosen to use the names that are most commonly used by the locals – sometimes it is English and sometimes Malay. Please note that the lowest two floors of multi-storey buildings are usually referred to as the ground floor (G/F) and the first floor (1/F). As the Chinese associate the number '4' with death, in some lifts, the fourth floor button is usually marked as '3A' instead.

B

Budgeting

KL is more expensive than the rest of the region except Singapore, but the budget-conscious will also find it manageable, particularly outside of peak season, which is the northern hemisphere summer. If you are frugal, you can get by on RM150 a day; RM250 per day is a fair budget. There is a 6 percent goods and services tax (GST) and some establishments also add an additional 10 percent service charge.

Decent budget accommodation can be found at around RM60; on average, RM400 gets you a room in a good 4-star hotel. Many hotels include breakfast with the room rate.

Street food is very cheap; a meal with a soft drink can be as low as RM10. Generally, budget RM40 for a main meal in a restaurant; Western food is more expensive. Alcohol is very expensive, with beers going for at least RM15 a pop, so do take advantage of happy hour rates. Entry to attractions run by the government is free or nominal, while privately-run attractions often charge hefty fees. Note that tourists pay up to twice the amounts charged to locals. Theatre tickets are generally reasonable, and matinee theatre shows are discounted. Go-KL buses in the city centre are free; trains are cheap and taxi fares are affordable. Car hire is reasonably priced, but parking in the city centre and in hotels is very expensive.

Business Hours

Government offices and some private businesses operate Monday–Friday 8.30am–5.30pm, with a one-hour lunch break from 12.30pm. There is a longer break from 12.45–2.45pm for Muslim prayers on Friday. Some companies also operate on Saturday 9am–1pm.

During the Muslim fasting month of Ramadan, government office hours are Monday–Thursday 8am–4.30pm and Friday 8am–4pm. Hours for private

MATIC at night

businesses vary, though most retain the same hours.

Banking hours are Monday–Friday 9.30am–4.30pm, although banks in shopping malls open at 10am and for a half-day on Saturday. Money-changing kiosks in the city are open until 7pm daily. Malls open daily 10am–10pm, even on public holidays.

Restaurants usually open from 11am–2.30pm and 5–11pm and have extended opening hours on weekends, unless they are in malls where they follow mall hours. *Mamak* outlets, that serve Indian and Malay food, are open 24 hours a day; some hawker places only open for dinner and don't close until 4am. Museums and art galleries open 10am–6pm but other attractions have longer opening hours.

Children

The city is not baby-friendly – facilities for breast-feeding, nappy-changing and pushchairs are inadequate to say the least. However, Malaysians love children and a helping hand with your stroller or carrier bags is never far away. Some hotels with 4 stars and above have kids' clubs, with activities and minders for children. Malls and fast-food outlets have play areas.

Children may be more susceptible to heat, food and water-related ailments. Always use sunblock, hats, insect repellent and drink lots of water. While pharmacies, such as Watsons and Guardian, are well stocked with children's medication, do bring along any special medication.

Climate

Malaysia's weather is generally hot and humid all year round, with temperatures ranging from 32°C (89.6°F) during the day to 22°C (71.6°F) at night. It is slightly colder in the highland areas, including Fraser's Hill and Genting Highlands. Humidity is at 80 percent; quick showers and thunderstorms occasionally occur. The heaviest rainfall is typically during the inter-monsoon periods of April to May and October to November. The months of January to March are hot and dry.

Thick haze is also an issue, which can appear anytime from July to October, with most of the smoke blown in from parts of Indonesia hit by forest fires (check the air pollution index at http://apims.doe.gov.my).

Weather patterns have become unpredictable. Check for more details with the Malaysian Meteorological Service (www.met.gov.my).

Clothing

Pack cottons and natural fibres, sunglasses, sunblock and umbrellas. Shoes are removed before one enters temples and homes, so slip-ons are handy. If you are planning on long-distance travel by bus or train, pack a jumper as the air-conditioning can be Arctic-like.

Royal Malaysia Police Museum

Crime and Security

Snatch and petty thefts are common. Snatch thieves tend to consist of two men on a motorcycle or men leaning out of moving cars. If your bag is snatched, give in, as many thieves carry knives, which they will not hesitate to use. Always walk in the direction of oncoming traffic and make sure your bag is on the side away from traffic. If you do not want to leave your valuables and passport in the hotel room safe, leave them with the reception. At night, keep to well-lit areas.

To contact the police, simply call 999. You can also get help at any police station or booth.

Customs

You must declare all prohibited and dutiable goods. The former includes drugs, dangerous chemicals, pornography, firearms and ammunition. Note that possession of drugs carries a death sentence. Items such as cameras, watches, pens, perfumes, cosmetics and lighters are duty free. You may have to pay a deposit for temporary importation of dutiable goods. This is refundable on departure (keep your receipt of purchase and get an official receipt for any tax or deposit paid). When you leave the country, you can also claim back GST for eligible goods. For details, call the **Customs Department** at tel: 1300-888-500; www.customs.gov.my.

Disabled travellers

Basic disabled-friendly facilities, like extra-wide parking bays and toilets, and wheelchair ramps, are found in major hotels, malls, theatres, fast-food restaurants and some government buildings. KLIA and the Light Rail Transit (LRT) system are also disabled-friendly. However in general, KL falls short with uneven pavements, potholes and unsympathetic drivers.

Electricity

Electrical outlets are rated at 220 volts, 50 cycles, and serve three-pinned, flat-pronged accessories. American products do not work here, but most supermarkets stock adapters. Major hotels will supply adaptors for 110–120 volt, 60 Hz appliances.

Embassies

Australia: 6 Jalan Yap Kwan Seng; tel: 03-2146 5555; www.malaysia.highcommission.gov.au

Canada: 17/F, Menara Tan & Tan, 207 Jalan Tun Razak; tel: 03-2718 3333; www.canadainternational.gc.ca/malaysia-malaisie/index.aspx?lang=eng

Ireland: The Amp Walk, 218 Jalan Ampang; tel: 03-2161 2963; www.dfa.ie/irish-embassy/malaysia/

New Zealand: 21/F, Menara IMC, 8

Jalan Sultan Ismail; tel: 03-2078 2533; www.mfat.govt.nz/en/countries-and-regions/south-east-asia/malaysia/new-zealand-high-commission/

UK: Level 27 Menara Binjai 2 Jalan Binjai; tel: 03-2170 2200; www.gov.uk/government/world/organisations/british-high-commission-kuala-lumpur

US: 376 Jalan Tun Razak; tel: 03-2168 5000; http://my.usembassy.gov

Emergencies

Police/Fire Brigade/Civil Defence: 999

Etiquette

Greetings: It is considered rude to address older people by their first names. Always use titles such as Mr (Encik), Madam (Puan) or Ms (Cik) or the more informal Pakcik/Uncle and Makcik/Aunty.

Men should not offer to shake a Muslim lady's hand unless she offers it first. A simple nod or smile will suffice. Similar rules apply to women wanting to shake a Muslim man's hand. A limp handshake is actually a Malay greeting (*salam*), which involves brushing the palm of the other person and placing the hand on one's heart. This signifies 'I am pleased to meet you from the bottom of my heart'.

Head & Feet: The Hindu religion regards the head as the wellspring of wisdom and the feet as unclean, so it is insulting to touch another adult's head, point one's feet at anything, or step over another person. Malays consider it rude to point the index finger at something;

make a fist with the right hand and the thumb folded on top, and then aim at the subject. If entering a home, remove your shoes. It is courteous to bring a gift, no matter how small. Never refuse drinks or snacks served to you, even if it is to take just a sip or bite. In a Malay home, when passing in front of someone, bow slightly while walking and point an arm down to indicate the path to be taken.

Places of Worship: Remove your shoes before entering temples and mosques. At the mosque, non-Muslims are prohibited from entering the main prayer hall; signs are clearly displayed. Conservative clothing covering arms and legs is advisable in mosques and some Hindu temples. Mosques there are popular with tourists will loan an over-garment and head covering for women.

If you enter a Sikh temple, be sure to cover your hair. Be sensitive about photographing worshippers in prayer.

Public Behaviour: Public displays of affection (other than hand-holding) are considered bad form. Shouting and talking loudly, even outside a nightspot, is considered rude.

Gay and lesbian travelers

KL has a sizeable gay community, unofficially estimated at 100,000. Malaysian society is generally tolerant of alternative lifestyles – though not of public dis-

plays of affection – and appreciative of the pink dollar. Gay visitors can travel safely and without fear of persecution in KL, usually facing only minor harassment from police, if at all. However, note that there are provisions in the Penal Code, and for Muslims, Islamic Shar'iah laws, that penalise same-sex sexual acts and cross-dressing.

Government

Malaysia is a constitutional monarchy with executive power vested in the prime minister and legislative power in an elected parliament. The government comprises a coalition of political parties (Barisan Nasional) that has ruled the country since independence. Since 2008, there has been a strong opposition presence in government. KL is a Federal Territory and the legislative capital of Malaysia; it is administered locally by a City Hall, led by a mayor.

H

Health

Visitors entering Malaysia are not required to show evidence of any vaccinations, but it is a good idea to immunise yourself against cholera, hepatitis A and B and tetanus; those above the age of 70 should get a flu shot. Bring all your own medications.

There are periodic outbreaks of dengue fever for which there is no immunisation, so take preventive measures like using insect repellent, especially at dawn and dusk. If you suffer from a very high fever while (or shortly after) visiting Malaysia, consult a doctor immediately. Check the latest news for pandemics that might be affecting Malaysia and take the necessary precautions. Note that the haze (see page 123) affects those with respiratory illnesses, especially asthmatics. Stay indoors or wear a mask when outdoors.

Make sure you drink at least 2 litres (8–10 glasses) of water to keep hydrated. Avoid the sun during the hottest part of the day (11am–1pm). Drink only boiled or bottled water. Avoid ice cubes at street side stalls and small coffee shops. Refrain from eating peeled fruit from street stalls. Otherwise, food served in restaurants and at hawker centres is clean.

Hospitals: All major hotels have an on-site clinic or a doctor-on-call. KL offers advanced medical care in both government and private hospitals. Government hospitals charge a fraction of what private ones demand, but there is usually a longer waiting time.

Hospital KL (government): Jalan Pahang; tel: 03-2615 5555; www.hkl.gov. my

University of Malaya Medical Centre (government): Lembah Pantai; tel: 03-7949 4222; www.ummc.edu.my

Tung Shin Hospital: Jalan Pudu (near Puduraya); tel: 03-2037 2288; www. tungshinhospital.com.my

Gleneagles Kuala Lumpur: Jalan Ampang; tel: 03-4141 3000; http://glen eagleskl.com.my

Malaysian flag on a bus

Medical Clinics: For minor problems, there are many private clinics around the city, some of which are open 24 hours.

Mediviron: throughout KL and Selangor; www.mediviron.com.my

Twin Towers Medical Clinic KLCC: KLCC and KL Sentral; http://ttmcklcc.com.my

Pharmacies: Pharmacies are found everywhere, especially in malls, usually operated by chains like Caring (www.caring2u.com), Watsons (www.watsons.com.my) and Guardian (www.guardian.com.my). A licensed pharmacist is usually on duty during office hours. A prescription is required for controlled drugs. Check the expiry dates.

Dental Clinics: Dental clinics are found in hospitals, major shopping malls and shopping areas like Bukit Bintang and the KLCC.

Dentalpro Dental Specialist Centre: 263 Jalan Maarof, Bangsar; tel: 03-2094 3333; www.dentalpro.org

Kuala Lumpur International Dental Centre; 33, 2/F, Jalan Yap Kwan Seng; tel: 03-2162 5555; http://www.klidc.com.my

Pristine Dental Clinic: F-074, 2/F, Mid Valley Megamall; tel: 03-2287 3782; http://pristinedental.com.my

Internet

Broadband internet access and wireless broadband (Wi-fi) are available in the city, airports and hotels of all categories. Coverage does tend to be worse outside the cities. Some hotels will charge for Internet access but in cafés, Wi-fi is usually free with the purchase of food or a drink; the cashier will give you a log-in name and password. You can also purchase data with a smartphone phone package at reasonable prices (see page 130)

L

Left Luggage

Hotels usually provide free left luggage services for their guests. **KLIA** and **KLIA2** (www.klia.com.my) provide storage services in the arrival halls. **KL Sentral** (www.stesensentral.com) has lockers on Levels 1 and 2. There are also left luggage services at **the Terminal Bersepadu Selatan** (TBS) interstate bus station on Level 3 (www.tbsbts.com.my).

Lost Property

If you have lost your property or passport, lodge a report at the nearest police station (www.rmp.gov.my). For lost property at KLIA, head to Level 2, Main Building (tel:03-8776 4312) and at KLIA2, Level 3, Departure Hall (tel: 03-8778 5409). For lost property at KL Sentral, call Information (tel: 03-2786 8260) and at TBS, call Customer Service (tel: 03-9051 2000).

M

Media

Newspapers/Magazines: Malaysia's English-language dailies include *The*

Newspaper stall

Star and *The New Straits Times*, tabloids such as *The Sun* and *Malay Mail*, and for business *The Edge* and the weekly *Focus Malaysia*. Popular online-only news portals include *Malaysiakini* (www.malaysiakini.com), *The Malay Mail Online* (www.themalaymailonline.com) and *FMT News* (www.freemalaysiatoday.com). Major hotels provide free local English-language dailies every morning, or you can purchase them at any bookshop or news-stand, where you can also buy selected international newspapers, periodicals and magazines. *Timeout KL* and *Essential KL* and are good for events and entertainment listings.

Radio: The premier talk radio station is BFM 98.8FM. English-language news is broadcast hourly on stations such as Hitz 92.9, which plays mainly American chart-toppers; Mix 94.5, which plays a mixture of new and old hits; and Light 105.7, which plays retro and classics. The government-run Traxx 90.3 airs a mix of music and talk shows.

Television: Cable TV, with channels such as CNN, BBC and HBO, is available in most hotels. Free-to-air local TV stations are run by RTM (TV1 and TV2) and by private stations TV3, NTV7 and TV9. All except for TV1 have news reports in English and largely American programmes. The paid satellite TV operator Astro has over 100 channels.

Money

Currency: The Malaysian ringgit (RM) is divided into 100 sen. Bank notes are in units of 1, 2, 5, 10, 50 and 100, and coins are in 5-, 10-, 20- and 50-sen denominations. Malaysians sometimes refer to ringgit and sen as 'dollars and cents'.

ATMs: These are located in banks, shopping areas centres and operate 6am–midnight but some international banks operate 24-hour machines. You can use your credit card to withdraw money from these machines.

Currency Exchange: Money-changers offer better rates than banks and are located everywhere, including the main bus and train terminals. Banks and Bureau de Change at KLIA charge a commission but money-changers do not. Try bargaining; larger amounts get you better rates.

Credit Cards: These are widely accepted but note that some retailers add an extra 3 percent surcharge, so ask first before paying. PINs are generally required. Be aware of credit card fraud. For lost cards call:

American Express: tel: 1800-88 9559
MasterCard: tel: 1800-804 594
Visa: tel: 1800-802 997

Taxes and Tipping: Most services are subject to a 10 percent service charge and a 6 percent government tax. Tipping is not compulsory but you may want to reward good service. Porters are tipped RM2–5, restaurant and bar staff are usually left loose change or change from bills rounded off to the nearest 10. Feel free to tip more for good service. Taxi drivers are usually not tipped.

Mosque rules

P

Photography

Camera shops are widely found in malls and tourist areas. Cameras and accessories are good bargains, as they are duty free here. Most photo-processing shops offer digital photo transfers onto DVDs and print services. For camera repairs and second-hand equipment, head to the Pudu area near Bukit Bintang. Likewise, video equipment and digital tapes are affordable.

Be prepared for rain and always have a plastic bag handy for your equipment. Note that the humidity in rainforest areas can damage cameras. Pack a dry non-lint cloth for wiping your camera. Although there are no restrictions on what you can photograph or video, use your discretion in religious places. When in doubt, ask for permission. Some attractions charge a fee for cameras.

Postal Services

Pos Malaysia (tel: 1300-300 300; www.pos.com.my) offers a gamut of services, including registered mail, parcels and courier services (Poslaju). Most post offices are open Monday–Friday 8am–5.30pm and until 1pm on Saturday. The **General Post Office** is at Kompleks Dayabumi. Post offices with extended hours from Monday to Saturday are in Bangsar (until 10pm), Mid Valley Megamall (until 9pm) and Sungei Wang Plaza (until 8pm). There is also a post office in the Main Building in KLIA.

International courier services include:
Federal Express (FedEx): The Weld Shopping Centre, Jalan Raja Chulan; tel: 1800-886 363; www.fedex.com; Mon–Fri 10am–7pm and Sat 10am–2pm.
Mail Boxes Etc **(UPS and DHL)**: Level 2M, Pavilion KL; tel: 03-2148 0380; www.mbe.com.my; daily 10am–10pm.

Public Holidays

Some holidays are fixed while others have variable dates as they are governed by the lunar calendar. Check specific dates with **Tourism Malaysia** (tel: 1300-885 050; www.malaysia.travel).
New Year's Day: 1 January
Thaipusam: end January
Federal Territory Day: 1 February
Chinese New Year: January/February
Labour Day: 1 May
Wesak Day: May
Agong's (King's) Birthday: first Saturday in June
National Day: 31 August
Malaysia Day: 16 September
Deepavali: October/November
Christmas: 25 December
Prophet Muhammad's Birthday: date variable
Hari Raya Puasa: date variable
Hari Raya Haji: date variable

R

Religion

As the majority of the population are Muslim, mosques are very common and

St Mary's Cathedral

all public buildings have at least a *surau* (prayer room). There are also ample places of worship for Buddhists, Taoists, Hindus, Sikhs and followers of other faiths. Of the various Christian denominations, here is a list of churches that offer English-language services.

Anglican: St Mary's Cathedral; Jalan Raja; tel: 03-2692 8672

Catholic: Cathedral of St John; 5 Jalan Bukit Nanas; tel: 03-2078 1876

Methodist: Wesley Methodist Church; 2 Jalan Wesley (near Puduraya); tel: 03-2072 0338

T

Telephones

Phone Numbers: IDD (International Direct Dial) phones are available in guest rooms. To call abroad directly, first dial the international access code 00, followed by the country code. Dial 103 for local and international telephone directory assistance and operator-assisted calls, dial 101. To call KL from overseas, dial the international country code 60 for Malaysia, followed by 3, the area code for KL and Selangor; 9 for Pahang.

Mobile Phones: Malaysia mobile phones use the GSM network. If your phone has a roaming facility, it will automatically hook up to a local network. Otherwise, prepaid SIM cards are very affordable, eg. for RM10, you get RM5 worth of calls valid for five days and 300MB data valid for 2 days. There's a mobile phone counter or shop at every corner; top-ups can also be done at 7-11 stores and petrol stations.

Toilets

Public restrooms can be dirty and wet, and many have squat toilets. Toilet paper is not always available, although you can sometimes buy small tissue packs at the entrance. Most malls charge an entrance fee of 50 sen. If you are concerned about hygiene, pop into a hotel to use its toilets.

Tourist Information

For detailed and comprehensive information including event listings and tour packages, visit the **Tourism Malaysia** website at www.malaysia.travel, or call 1300-885 050. Tourist offices have helpful staff and ample brochures and maps.

KLIA: Arrival Hall, Main Building; tel: 03-8776 4720; daily 24 hours

KLIA2: Arrival Level, Public Concourse; tel: 03-8778 7080; daily 24 hours

Malaysia Tourism Centre: 109 Jalan Ampang; tel: 03-9235 4848; www. matic.gov.my; daily 8am–10pm

Bangunan Sultan Abdul Samad: Jalan Raja; tel: 03-2602 2014; daily 9am–6pm

KL Sentral: 1/F, Arrival Halls, Kuala Lumpur City Air Terminal; daily 9am–6pm; tel: 03-2272 5823

Overseas Offices

Australia: Level 6, 151 Castlereagh Street, Sydney; tel: 61-2-9286 3055; Level 5, 150 St Georges Terrace, Perth

Thean Hou Temple

tel: +618-9481 0400

UK: 57 Trafalgar Square, London; tel: 44-20-7930 7932

US: 120 East, 56th Street, New York; tel: 1-212-754 1113; 818 West Seventh Street, Suite 970, Los Angeles; tel: 1-213-689-9702

For a full list of offices, visit www.malaysia.travel.

Tours

The Hop On-Hop Off (tel: 03-9282 2713; daily 9am–8pm; www.myhoponhopoff.com/kl) is a flexible tour that lets you see the main sights.

Plying 23 stops around the city, this double-decker bus service runs every 30–45 minutes and you can get on and off the bus at any of the designated stops along the way. Pre-recorded commentary is available on the bus.

Most hotels offer their own shuttle bus or van tours around the city. Some might not be licensed, so ask your hotel concierge or the reception desk to recommend a reliable tour company. Half-day 3-hour city tours are priced at around RM200 per person. Full-day tours of 8 hours cost RM600 per person. Individual tour guides charge a per-hour fee upwards of RM150. Be sure to use the services of a licensed guide. Check out the Malaysian Tourist Guides Council homepage (http://mtgc.my).

The following tour agencies offer tours of KL and its environs as well as longer and more comprehensive tours of various destinations in Malaysia.

Exotic Asia Holidays Travel & Tours: tel: 013-2084 862; www.kualalumpurtours.com.my

Holiday Tours: tel: 03-6286 6286; www.holidaytours.com.my

Kuala Lumpur Tour: tel: 012-2065071; www.kualalumpurtour.net

Mayflower Holidays: tel: 03-9232 1888; www.mayflower.com.my

Seri Malaya Travel & Tours: tel: 012-5080 479; www.serimalayatravel.com

Specialist tours such as walking, cycling and food tours are offered by small outfits. They tend not to be licensed for tourist guiding but are registered as businesses. Check online for reviews, ensure you have booking confirmations in writing and ask questions until you are satisfied:

Be Tourist (walking/food tours): tel: 03-2032 1031; www.malaysiaheritage.net Food Tour Malaysia (walking or driving food tours): tel: 013-227 1505; www.foodtourmalaysia.com

Putrajaya Rides (bicycle tours only in Putrajaya but they are looking at expanding): www.putrajayarides.com

Transport

Arrival

By Air: KL is serviced by three airports. The main airport is the **Kuala Lumpur International Airport**, or KLIA (tel: 03-8776 2000 3136/3145; www.klia.com.my), located 70km (43 miles) south of the city in Sepang. Planes arrive at and depart from four satellite arms, which are linked to the main terminal

building via an aerotrain with departures at 3–5-minute intervals. The national carrier is **Malaysia Airlines** (MH; 24-hour call centre tel: 03-7843 3000 or 1300-883 000 toll-free within Malaysia; www.malaysiaairlines.com), which flies to over 100 international and domestic destinations.

The budget airport is **KLIA2** (tel: 03-8778 5500 x 01/02/03; www.klia.com.my), located 10 minutes by car from KLIA; there are shuttles connecting the two every 20 minutes but if you end up at the wrong airport, getting a taxi is the fastest solution. This is a huge airport which requires a lot of walking, so ensure you get there early for flights. This is the airport for budget airline **AirAsia** (tel: 1600 85 8888; Mon–Fri 9am–6pm, toll-free within Malaysia; www.airasia.com) offers cheap fares to both domestic and regional destinations.

The third airport is the tiny **Sultan Abdul Aziz Shah Airport**, better known as **Subang Aiport**, 20km (12½ miles) from KL (tel: 03-7845 3245). MH subsidiary **Firefly**, operates from here, flying small Fokker 50 planes to selected local destinations (tel: 03-7845 4543; daily 8am–9pm; www.fireflyz.com.my).

Airport Transfers: The fastest way from KLIA and KLIA2 to the city centre is by the **KLIA Ekspres** train (daily 5am–1am; tel: 03-2267 8000 (Mon–Fri 8.30am–6pm); www.kliaekspres.com), which takes roughly 30 minutes to get to the KL Sentral station (RM55).

If you are flying with MH, Cathay Pacific, Emirates or Royal Brunei for the return trip, you can do a flight check-in, including luggage, at the **Central Air Terminal** (CAT) at KL Sentral 2–12 hours before departure. Alternative transport modes are **Airport Limo** taxis (tel: 03-8787 3678; 24 hours; buy a coupon before leaving the arrival hall), budget taxis using meters (from the basement) and **Airport Coach** (tel: 03-8787 3894; www.airportcoach.com.my; daily 5.30am–12.30am). **Jetbus** (tel: 019-221 6763; www.jetbus.com.my; daily 4.15am–12.45am) ferries passengers from both KLIA and KLIA2 to the TBS for interstate bus connections.

From KLIA2, the very affordable **Skybus** (tel: 016-217 8496; www.skybus.com.my; daily 5am–2.45am) and Aerobus (tel: 010-292 3888; www.aerobus.my; daily 4.30am–midnight) go to KL Sentral. Airport taxis go anywhere (tel: 03-8787 4113; 24 hours; buy a coupon before leaving the arrival hall), likewise, budget taxis using meters.

By Rail: The main train line from Singapore to Bangkok and beyond stops at the KL Sentral station. The **KTMB** (National Railways; tel: 03-2267 1200; www.ktmb.com.my) trains are modern and the service is efficient. Travellers generally take the express services, which make a minimal number of stops. There are three classes of service. Most trains are air-conditioned and have buffet cars serving simple meals. Comfort-

able sleeping berths are available on long-distance night trains.

There are day and night trains to both Singapore and Butterworth in Penang. From Butterworth, there are train connections to Thailand.

By Road: The North-South Expressway, which stretches from southern Peninsular Malaysia to the Thai border, provides a convenient means of travel through the peninsula, the entire trip taking about 12 hours by car one way. There are two links from Singapore: across the Causeway from Woodlands to Johor Bahru, and Linkedua (Second Link) from Tuas to Tanjung Kupang. Try to avoid crossing the border on Friday afternoons and during public holidays because the traffic can be heavy at the checkpoints.

Long-distance buses also travel to and from KL to most destinations on the peninsula as well as to Singapore and Thailand. Travel by air-conditioned express buses is comfortable, with video entertainment on board. The buses make occasional stops along the expressway for meals and toilet breaks.

The main interstate bus station is at the **Terminal Bersepadu Selatan** (TBS; tel: 03-9051 2000; www.tbsbts. com.my) 15km (9 miles) south of the city centre. From there, you can take the LRT, KTM Komuter or KLIA Transit to your KL destination. **The Nice brand of luxury coaches** (tel: 013-220 7867; www.nice-coaches.com.my) picks and drops passengers at the Old KL Rail-

way Station and KL Sentral for travel to Penang and Singapore.

By Sea: KL's closest seaport is **Port Klang** (Pelabuhan Klang), about 40km (25 miles) away, and is linked by highways, buses and the KTM Komuter train service. Ferries from Tanjung Balai (tel: 03-3165 2545) and Dumai (www. tunasrupat.com), Sumatra (in Indonesia) dock here. Port Klang is the main port of call for regional cruise ships and international liners.

Within KL

Taxis: Taxis have a 'Teksi' sign on their roofs, which, when lit, signals availability. They offer a convenient and economical means of moving around the city, and drivers usually speak at least a smattering of English.

Air-conditioning and fare meters are compulsory in all taxis. Make sure the meter is switched on after you get in. Rates are RM3 for the first 2km (1.24 miles) and 25 sen for each additional 200 metres. Tolls are paid by passengers and there is a surcharge of RM2 for booking a taxi by phone, and a 50 percent surcharge on the meter fare between midnight and 6am. There are also premium taxis that have a RM4 flagfall and charge more per kilometre (check the latest rates at www.spad. gov.my).

You can get a taxi by queuing at taxi stands or flagging one down by the street. However, taxis in tourist areas are notorious for over-charging, so

KL Monorail

avoid this by using smartphone apps such as Grab, Uber and Ezcab, which stipulate the chargeable fares and provide recourse for complaints. Grab and Ezcab have licensed taxi drivers signed up as well; these are more ethical than street taxis and the cabs are also in a better condition. This service has a RM2 levy. Some tourist attractions, airports and KL Sentral have coupon taxis for which you pre-pay.

Half- and full-day taxi charters around Klang Valley cost RM30 per hour, excluding toll charges; travelling further incurs a petrol levy.

Buses: Several companies provide bus services in KL between 6am and 11pm. Buses are air-conditioned and modern and fares cheap, but timetables are not adhered to. You can pay cash or buy a Touch n Go card (http://touchngo.com. my) which you can use on most public transport. Buses are packed during peak periods; watch your belongings.

GoKL (tel: 1-800-88-7723; www. gokl.com.my) is a free city bus service within the central business district that goes to most tourist attractions. The main interchange is in Bukit Bintang (Pavilion/Starhill).

Rapid KL's **City Shuttle** buses (tel: 03-7885 2585; www.myrapidkl.com. my) will take you out to Petaling Jaya and Klang.

Rail: Travelling on the modern, air-conditioned trains are the best way to avoid traffic jams. Trains run on average every 7–8 minutes (every

3 minutes during peak hours) from 6am–midnight. You can pay cash or use the Touch n Go card.

But KL has a confusing number of rail systems, not all of which connect to each other, other than at the central transport hub of Stesen Sentral Kuala Lumpur, better known as **KL Sentral** (tel: 03-2786 8260; www.stesen sentral.com).

Within the city, **Rapid KL** (tel: 03-7885 2585; www.rapidkl.com.my) operates two systems. The Light Rail Transport (LRT) has two lines that intersect at Masjid Jamek and services areas such as the Golden Triangle, the old city centre, Petaling Jaya and Bangsar. The **Monorail** covers the Bukit Bintang, Brickfields and Titiwangsa areas.

The **KTM Komuter** (tel: 03-2267 1200; www.ktmb.com.my) electric commuter rail service transports commuters and travellers on two lines throughout the Klang Valley.

The newest system, which is being built, is the **Mass Rapid Transport** (MRT; tel: 1800-826 868; www.mymrt. com.my). It has three lines that will cut through and link with all of the above.

Rental Cars: Driving in the city is unwise because of traffic jams and ill-mannered drivers but driving outside of the city is a pleasure, with wide highways and lovely scenery. You will need to have cash handy for tolls or buy a Touch n Go card, which you can also use on public transport. You need an international driver's licence unless you are from the US, EU,

The Kelana Jaya line

Australia, New Zealand, Japan and Singapore (double-check the Road Transport Department's page www.jpj.gov.my/web/eng/acceptance-of-foreign-driving-license). Rental rates vary according to insurance options and vehicle type, but generally start at RM150 per day plus third-party insurance. Most car hire companies have outlets in airports including: **Avis** (www.avis.com.my), **Kasina Rent-A-Car** (http://kasina.com.my), **Malyflower Car Rental** (www.mayflowercarrental.com.my) and **Hertz** (www.hertz.com).

Visas and Passports

Passports must be valid for at least six months at the time of entry. Visa requirements change from time to time, so check with a Malaysian embassy or consulate or the **Immigration Department** website (www.imi.gov.my) before travelling. Generally, no visa is needed for citizens of Commonwealth countries (with exceptions), the US and most EU countries (up to three months); and all ASEAN countries except Myanmar and some EU countries (up to one month).

Websites

Badan Warisan Malaysia: http://badanwarisanmalaysia.org. Information about history and heritage.

EDMDroid: www.edmdroid.com. News and listings on nightlife in KL and the region, including a list of DJs.

KY Speaks: http://kyspeaks.com. Reviews of and guide to food in KL and elsewhere.

Journeymalaysia: www.journeymalaysia.com. Comprehensive information related to travel.

Kakiseni: www.kakiseni.com. Community-seeded listings of arts events, classes and workshops.

Loyar Buruk: www.loyarburok.com. A sounding board for left-leaning activism-based bloggers.

Says: http://says.com. The 'it' Malaysian social media news and story aggregator.

Timeout Kuala Lumpur: www.timeout.com/kuala-lumpur. Comprehensive listings of what's on and what's hot.

Women Travelers

It is generally safe for women to travel alone in KL. If you don't want being hassled, just wear a wedding band, or say, 'Yes, I'm married,' in reply to queries on your marriage status. With unsolicited attention, be polite but firm and walk away if you are uncomfortable. You should dress more conservatively in places of worship and outside the city. Topless bathing at swimming pools is prohibited.

LANGUAGE

Most people in Kuala Lumpur are at least bilingual and speak some to native-level English. On the street, you will hear colourful localised forms of English, which may sound ungrammatical, but has a unique phonology, syntax, grammar and vocabulary, and borrows liberally from local languages and for migrant workers, their own languages. For instance, 'Came from where?' is 'Where did you just come from?'; 'They already *makan*' means 'They have already eaten'.

Malay or Bahasa Malaysia is the national language and lingua franca. It is also spoken in Singapore, Indonesia, the Philippines, Brunei and southern Thailand. In schools and formal settings, a standardised form of Malay is used. Regional dialects exist and may not be mutually intelligible – a KL-ite may not understand Bahasa from Kelantan.

As all public signboards are in Malay, it is useful to know some common words. Malay is not a difficult language to learn. Words from other languages, including English, Sanskrit, Arabic, Chinese, Portuguese, Dutch and Thai, have been incorporated into the Malay vocabulary.

Numbers

Satu **1**
Dua **2**
Tiga **3**
Empat **4**
Lima **5**
Enam **6**
Tujuh **7**
Lapan **8**
Sembilan **9**
Sepuluh **10**
Sebelas **11**
Dua belas **12**
Dua puluh **20**
Dua puluh satu **21**
Seratus **100**
Dua ratus **200**
Seribu **1,000**
Dua ribu **2,000**

Pronouns

Saya/Aku **I/Me**
Anda/Awak/Kamu **You**
Dia **He/She**
Kita **We (inclusive of person being addressed)**
Kami **We (exclusive of person being addressed)**
Mereka **They**

Days of the week

Isnin **Monday**
Selasa **Tuesday**
Rabu **Wednesday**
Khamis **Thursday**
Jumaat **Friday**
Sabtu **Saturday**
Ahad **Sunday**

Directions

Pergi **Go**

Office workers in conversation

Berhenti **Stop**
Belok **Turn**
Kiri **Left**
Kanan **Right**
Hadapan **Forward/Front**
Belakang **Behind**
Keluar **Exit**
Masuk **Enter**
Dekat **Near**
Jauh **Far**
Dalam **Inside**
Luar **Outside**
Sini **Here**
Sana **There**
Utara **North**
Selatan **South**
Timur **East**
Barat **West**

Other phrases

Apa khabar? **How do you do?**
Selamat pagi **Good morning**
Selamat tengah hari **Good afternoon**
Selamat petang **Good evening**
Selamat malam **Good night**
Selamat tinggal **Goodbye**
Tolong/sila **Please**
Maafkan saya **Excuse me**
Siapa nama anda? **What is your name?**
Nama saya **My name is**
Minta maaf **I apologise**
Terima kasih **Thank you**
Sama-sama **You're welcome**
Berapa harganya? **How much is it?**
Terlalu mahal **Too expensive**
Kurangkan harga **Lower the price**
Terlalu besar **Too big**
Terlalu kecil **Too small**

At the restaurant

Minum **Drink**
Makan **Eat**
Air (pronounced a-yir) **Water**
Pedas **Hot (spicy)**
Panas **Hot (heat)**
Sejuk **Cold**
Suam **Warm (water)**
Manis **Sweet**
Masam **Sour**
Masin **Salty**
Sedap **Delicious**
Bread *Roti*
Rice *Nasi*
Noodles *Mee*
Vegetables *Sayur*
Chicken *Ayam*
Pork *Babi*
Beef *Daging (also means 'meat')*
Fish *Ikan*
I'm vegetarian *Saya makan sayur saja*
Not spicy/sweet/etc *Tak mahu pedas/ manis/etc*
Less spicy/sweet/etc *Kurang pedas/ manis etc*

Other words

Cantik **Beautiful**
Sedikit **A little**
Banyak **A lot**
Ini **This**
Itu **That**
Bersih **Clean**
Kotor **Dirty**
Buka **Open**
Tutup **Close**
Duit **Money**
Duit kecil **Spare change**

Bookshop in Shah Alam

BOOKS AND FILM

Malaysians are not big readers other than of self-improvement and cookery books. This is not to say that Malaysians don't write. In literature, first-generation poets and writers in English like Adibah Amin, K.S. Maniam, Lloyd Fernando, and Salleh Joned are products of the post-colonial landscape, independence and the ensuing political and social climates. Today's writers focus on identity including ethnicity, religion, gender, and regional origin in a plural Malaysian society. Malay and English-language literary writing is booming through the efforts of small publishing firms, and the attention that notable Malaysian authors have garnered internationally.

In film, Malay-language pulp cinema featuring romance, ghosts and gangsters is huge in Malaysia but it is the high-quality indie films that are worth watching. The golden age of cinema was in the 1950s and 60s with the multi-talented P. Ramlee as its illustrious icon. The noughties saw Malaysian New Wave auteurs make inroads into the international film-festival circuit in Malay, Mandarin and English. Yasmin Ahmad was Malaysia's most influential contemporary filmmaker, using both commercials and features to attempt depicting realistic inter-ethnic worlds. Producing short films continues to be the pathway to feature films, many of which are excellent.

Books

History, Politics and Economy
A History of Malaysia, by Barbara Watson Andaya and Leonard Y Andaya. Traces how modern Malaysia was shaped by cultural heritage and trade.

Malaysia's Political Economy, by Edmund Terence Gomez and KS Jomo. These top economists provide an accessible analysis of the relationship between contemporary business and politics.

The End of Empire, by TN Harper. A thoughtful analysis of how Malaya was created by a plural society caught in crisis.

Cookery
The Little Malaysian Cookbook, by Wendy Hutton. Nasi lemak, Hainanese chicken rice and satay are just some of the recipes in this book of Malaysia's favourite hawker fare.

Malaysian Cooking: ***A Master Cook Reveals Her Best Recipes***, by Carol Selvarajah. This reprint of a book by a household name captures the Malaysian kitchen in easy-to-follow recipes.

Natural History
Natural History Drawings: The Complete William Farquhar Collection, Malay Peninsula 1803–1818. Evocative colonial-era watercolours bring 477 species to life, accompanied by essays and detailed captions.

A scene from Flower in the Pocket, 2007

Wild Malaysia: The Wildlife, Scenery, and Biodiversity of Peninsular Malaysia, Sabah, and Sarawak, by Geoffrey Davidson, et al. A beautifully photographed hardcover book on the country's natural history.

Fiction

Sejarah Melayu (The Malay Annals). Dating back to the 14th century, this is one of the finest Malay historical literary works, and depicts a romanticised history of the great Malay maritime empire of Melaka.

The Harmony Silk Factory, by Tash Aw. A superbly crafted tale of a dysfunctional family told in three narrative voice and deft weaving in of British Malaya history and culture.

Evening is the Whole Day, by Preeta Samarasan. An atmospheric tale set in the 1980s about family, race and class revolving around a Malaysian Indian family.

General

Kuala Lumpur - a sketchbook, by Chin Yon Kit and Chen Voon Fee. Annotated collection of beautiful watercolour paintings of old KL's built architecture.

The Kampung Boy, by Lat. This beloved classic graphic novel is written and drawn by Malaysia's top cartoonist and is drawn from Lat's own experiences growing up in a kampung (village).

Born in Malaysia: a Photographer's Journey, by Kenny Loh & Tan Joo Lee. From shopkeepers to fisherfolk and hawkers, this book is a pictorial tribute to the lives and livelihoods.

Masam-Masam Manis (**Sweet-Sou**r, 1965). This classic romantic comedy by P Ramlee about a teacher who moonlights as a saxophone player, features KL heavily.

The Big Durian (2003). Amir Muhammad's powerful political documentary feature tackles Malaysia's security laws and crackdowns.

The Beautiful Washing Machine (2004). It's about a washing machine, a metaphorical view of alienation and desperation in KL by James Lee. (Mandarin)

Love Conquers All (2007). Big city life in KL seduces a young woman in Tan Chui Mui's intimate narrative. (Mandarin)

Flower in the Pocket (2007). An endearing film about an emotionally absent father and his two sons is by the award-winning Liew Seng Tat. (Mandarin)

Karaoke (2009). Nominated for the Cannes Film Festival Camera d'Or, Chris Chong's arty languorous film is about a young man who makes karaoke videos. (Malay)

Bunohan (Return to Murder, 2012). Dain Said's Lear-like film about betrayal pairs kick-boxing with traditional shadow-puppetry, and drips with atmosphere. (Kelantanese Malay)

Terbaik Dari Langit (2014). This is a quirky comedy-drama about pursuing a UFO; in the process, childhood relationships are tested. (Malay)

ABOUT THIS BOOK

This *Explore Guide* has been produced by the editors of Insight Guides, whose books have set the standard for visual travel guides since 1970. With top-quality photography and authoritative recommendations, these guidebooks bring you the very best routes and itineraries in the world's most exciting destinations.

BEST ROUTES

The routes in the book provide something to suit all budgets, tastes and trip lengths. As well as covering the destination's many classic attractions, the itineraries track lesser-known sights, and there are also ex-cursions for those who want to extend their visit outside the city. The routes embrace a range of interests, so whether you are an art fan, a gourmet, a history buff or have kids to entertain, you will find an option to suit.

We recommend reading the whole of a route before setting out. This should help you to familiarise yourself with it and enable you to plan where to stop for refreshments – options are shown in the 'Food and Drink' box at the end of each tour.

For our pick of the tours by theme, consult Recommended Routes for… (see pages 6–7).

INTRODUCTION

The routes are set in context by this introductory section, giving an overview of the destination to set the scene, plus background information on food and drink, shopping and more, while a succinct history timeline highlights the key events over the centuries.

DIRECTORY

Also supporting the routes is a Directory chapter, with a clearly organised A–Z of practical information, our pick of where to stay while you are there and select restaurant listings; these eateries complement the more low-key cafés and restaurants that feature within the routes and are intended to offer a wider choice for evening dining. Also included here are some nightlife listings, plus a handy language guide and our recommendations for books and films about the destination.

ABOUT THE AUTHOR

SL Wong is a Malaysia-born freelance writer who has used Kuala Lumpur as her base for two decades. Having lived in Australia, Singapore, Hong Kong and Germany, she loves KL's eclectic blend of Asian chaos and globalised influences. Day and night, for work and for play, she thrives on the energy from the city's multifarious cultures, inherited traditions and quirky charms. She adores the food and when she needs to, finds escape from urban frenzy a short drive away in the charms of rural life and the restorative energy of primeval rainforests.

CONTACT THE EDITORS

We hope you find this Explore Guide useful, interesting and a pleasure to read. If you have any questions or feedback on the text, pictures or maps, please do let us know. If you have noticed any errors or outdated facts, or have suggestions for places to include on the routes, we would be delighted to hear from you. Please drop us an email at hello@insightguides.com. Thanks!

CREDITS

Explore Kuala Lumpur
Editor: Tom Fleming
Author: Siew Lyn Wong
Head of Production: Rebeka Davies
Update Production: Apa Digital
Picture Editor: Tom Smyth
Cartography: Carte
Photo credits: Alamy 23L, 73, 139; Getty Images 4/5T, 22, 27, 93L, 92/93, 95; Hilton Hotels & Resorts 106, 109, 119; Hyatt 100/101T, 104; iStock 6ML, 14/15T, 28/29T, 42/43, 68, 80, 81L; James Tye/ Apa Publications 4ML, 4MR, 4MR, 4MC, 4ML, 7MR, 8ML, 8MC, 8MR, 8/9T, 12B, 12T, 13L, 12/13, 16, 17L, 25L, 32/33, 36/37, 38, 38/39, 40, 50/51T, 52B, 52T, 54/55, 64, 67, 69L, 68/69, 70, 71, 82, 83, 115, 117, 122, 126, 127, 128, 129, 132, 133, 137; Jon Santa Cruz/ Apa Publications 61, 62; Nikt Wong/Apa Publications 21L, 22/23, 26, 55L, 56, 58, 59L, 58/59, 74, 75L, 74/75, 78, 78/79, 84, 86, 87L, 86/87, 88, 89L, 88/89, 94; Shangri-La International 8MR, 100ML, 105, 112, 113, 120/121; Shutterstock 7M, 79L, 80/81, 85, 91, 96, 108, 138; SuperStock 19, 30/31; Tourism Malaysia 1, 4MC, 6TL, 6MC, 6BC, 7T, 7MR, 8ML, 8MC, 10, 11B, 11T, 14B, 16/17, 18, 20, 20/21, 24, 24/25, 28ML, 28MC, 28MR, 28ML, 28MC, 28MR, 30, 31L, 32B, 32T, 33L, 34/35, 36, 37L, 39L, 41, 42B, 42T, 43L, 44, 45B, 45T, 46B, 46T, 47, 48, 49L, 48/49, 50, 50/51M, 51T, 53, 54, 57, 60, 63, 65L, 64/65, 66, 72, 76, 77, 90, 92, 97, 98, 99L, 98/99, 100MR, 100MR, 111, 114, 116, 118, 123, 124, 125, 130, 131, 134, 135, 136; YTL Hotels 100ML, 100MC, 100MC, 102, 103, 107, 110
Cover credits: Shutterstock (main&bottom)

Printed by CTPS – China

First Edition 2017

DISTRIBUTION

UK, Ireland and Europe
Apa Publications (UK) Ltd
sales@insightguides.com
United States and Canada
Ingram Publisher Services
ips@ingramcontent.com
Australia and New Zealand
Woodslane
info@woodslane.com.au
Southeast Asia
Apa Publications (Singapore) Pte
singaporeoffice@insightguides.com
Hong Kong, Taiwan and China
Apa Publications (HK) Ltd
hongkongoffice@insightguides.com
Worldwide
Apa Publications (UK) Ltd
sales@insightguides.com

SPECIAL SALES, CONTENT LICENSING AND COPUBLISHING

Insight Guides can be purchased in bulk quantities at discounted prices. We can create special editions, personalised jackets and corporate imprints tailored to your needs.
sales@insightguides.com
www.insightguides.biz

INDEX

MAP LEGEND

●	Start of tour
→	Tour & route direction
❶	Recommended sight
❷	Recommended restaurant/café
★	Place of interest
❶	Tourist information
✈	Airport

⊷⊷	Railway
═══	Motorway
- - -	Ferry route
🚌	Main bus station
Ⓜ	Metro station
✉	Main post office
⚲	Statue/monument
🏛	Museum/gallery

🎭	Theatre
⊡ †	Church
▬	Important building
▭	Park
▭	Urban area
▭	Non-urban area
▬	Shop / market
▨	Transport hub